CONVERSATIONS
WITH SCRIPTURE:
ROMANS

Other Books in the Series

CONVERSATIONS WITH SCRIPTURE:

ROMANS

JAY SIDEBOTHAM

Morehouse Publishing
NEW YORK

Unless otherwise noted, the Scripture quotations contained herein are from the New Revised Standard Version Bible, copyright © 1989 by the Division of Christian Education of the National Council of Churches of Christ in the U.S.A. Used by permission. All rights reserved.

Scripture references marked (KJV) are taken from the Authorized King James Version of the Holy Bible.

Morehouse Publishing, 19 East 34th Street, New York, NY 10016

Morehouse Publishing is an imprint of Church Publishing Incorporated.
www.churchpublishing.org

Cover art: Alexsol/istock/Thinkstock

Series cover design by Corey Kent

Series design by Beth Oberholtzer

Library of Congress Cataloging-in-Publication Data

Sidebotham, Jay.
    Conversation with scripture : Romans / Jay Sidebotham.
      pages cm
    Includes bibliographical references.
    ISBN 978-0-8192-2991-5 (pbk.) — ISBN 978-0-8192-2992-2 (ebook)
    1. Bible. Romans—Commentaries. I. Title.
BS2665.53.S53 2015
227'.107—dc23

                                      2014042796

Printed in the United States of America

This book is dedicated to John Murchison,
who shows grace because he knows grace.

CONTENTS

INTRODUCTION
TO THE SERIES

To talk about a distinctively Anglican approach to Scripture is a daunting task. Within any one part of the larger church that we call the Anglican Communion there is, on historical grounds alone, an enormous variety. But as the global character of the church becomes apparent in ever-newer ways, the task of accounting for that variety, while naming the characteristics of a distinctive approach becomes increasingly difficult.

In addition, the examination of Scripture is not confined to formal studies of the kind addressed in this series of parish studies written by formally trained biblical scholars. Systematic theologian David Ford, who participated in the Lambeth Conference of 1998, rightly noted that although "most of us have studied the Bible over many years" and "are aware of various academic approaches to it," we have "also lived in it" and "inhabited it, through worship, preaching, teaching and meditation." As such, Ford observes, "The Bible in the Church is like a city we have lived in for a long time." We may not be able to account for the history of every building or the architecture on every street, but we know our way around and it is a source of life to each of us.[1]

That said, we have not done as much as we should in acquainting the inhabitants of that famed city with the architecture that lies within. So, as risky as it may seem, it is important to set out an introduction to the highlights of that city—which this series proposes to explore at length. Perhaps the best way in which to broach that task is to provide a handful of descriptors.

The first of those descriptors that leaps to mind is familiar, basic, and forever debated: *authoritative*. Years ago I was asked by a colleague who belonged to the Evangelical Free Church why someone with as much obvious interest in the Bible would be an Episcopal priest. I responded, "Because we read the whole of Scripture and not just the parts of it that suit us." Scripture has been and continues to play a singular role in the life of the Anglican Communion, but it has rarely been used in the sharply prescriptive fashion that has characterized some traditions.

Some have characterized this approach as an attempt to navigate a *via media* between overbearing control and an absence of accountability. But I think it is far more helpful to describe the tensions not as a matter of steering a course between two different and competing priorities, but as the complex dance necessary to live under a very different, but typically Anglican notion of authority itself. Authority shares the same root as the word "to author" and as such, refers first and foremost, not to the *power* to *control* with all that both of those words suggest, but to the capacity to *author creativity*, with all that both of those words suggest.[2] As such, the function of Scripture is to carve out a creative space in which the work of the Holy Spirit can yield the very kind of fruit associated with its work in the Church. The difficulty, of course, is that for that space to be creative, it is also necessary for it to have boundaries, much like the boundaries we establish for other kinds of genuinely creative freedom—the practice of scales for concert pianists, the discipline of work at the barré that frees the ballerina, or the guidance that parents provide for their children. Defined in this way, it is possible to see the boundaries around that creative space as barriers to be eliminated, or as walls that provide protection, but they are neither.

And so the struggle continues with the authority of Scripture. From time to time in the Anglican Communion, it has been and will be treated as a wall that protects us from the complexity of navigating without error the world in which we live. At other times, it will be treated as the ancient remains of a city to be cleared away in favor of a brave new world. But both approaches are rooted, not in the limitations of Scripture, but in our failure to welcome the creative space we have been given.

For that reason, at their best, Anglican approaches to Scripture are also *illuminative*. William Sloane Coffin once observed that the problem with Americans and the Bible is that we read it like a drunk uses a lamppost. We lean on it, we don't use it for illumination.[3] Leaning on Scripture—or having the lamppost taken out completely—are simply two very closely related ways of failing to acknowledge the creative space provided by Scripture. But once the creative space is recognized for what it is, then the importance of reading Scripture illuminatively becomes apparent. Application of the insight Scripture provides into who we are and what we might become is not something that can be prescribed or mapped out in detail. It is only a conversation with Scripture, marked by humility that can begin to spell out the particulars. Reading Scripture is, then, in the Anglican tradition a delicate and demanding task, that involves both the careful listening for the voice of God and courageous conversation with the world around us.

It is, for that reason, an approach that is also marked by *critical engagement* with the text itself. It is no accident that from 1860 to 1900 the three best-known names in the world of biblical scholarship were Anglican priests, the first two of whom were Bishops: B. F. Westcott, J. B. Lightfoot, and F. J. A. Hort. Together the three made contributions to both the church and the critical study of the biblical text that became a defining characteristic of Anglican life.

Of the three, Westcott's contribution, perhaps, best captures the balance. Not only did his work contribute to a critical text of the Greek New Testament that would eventually serve as the basis for the English Revised Version, but as Bishop of Durham he also convened a conference of Christians to discuss the arms race in Europe, founded the Christian Social Union, and mediated the Durham coal strike of 1892.

The English roots of the tradition are not the only, or even the defining characteristic of Anglican approaches to Scripture. The church, no less than the rest of the world, has been forever changed by the process of globalization, which has yielded a rich *diversity* that complements the traditions once identified with the church.

Scripture in Uganda, for example, has been read with an emphasis on private, allegorical, and revivalist applications. The result has been a tradition in large parts of East Africa which stresses the reading of Scripture on one's own; the direct application made to the contemporary situation without reference to the setting of the original text; and the combination of personal testimony with the power of public exhortation.

At the same time, however, globalization has brought that tradition into conversation with people from other parts of the Anglican Communion as the church in Uganda has sought to bring the biblical text to bear on its efforts to address the issues of justice, poverty, war, disease, food shortage, and education. In such a dynamic environment, the only thing that one can say with certainty is that neither the Anglican Communion, nor the churches of East Africa, will ever be the same again.

Authoritative, illuminative, critical, and varied—these are not the labels that one uses to carve out an approach to Scripture that can be predicted with any kind of certainty. Indeed, if the word *dynamic*—just used—is added to the list, perhaps all that one can predict is still more change! And, for that reason, there will be observers who (not without reason) will argue that the single common denominator in this series is that each of the authors also happens to be an Anglican. (There might even be a few who will dispute that!)

But such is the nature of life in any city, including one shaped by the Bible. We influence the shape of its life, but we are also shaped and nurtured by it. And if that city is of God's making, then to force our own design on the streets and buildings around us is to disregard the design that the chief architect has in mind.

—Frederick W. Schmidt
Series Editor

When Dr. William Willimon was serving as chaplain at Duke University, a professor from a local college approached him with an observation about church: "It's just that I don't see anything different or special about what we do on Sunday in church, and what's going on at any number of other very helpful organizations. Friendliness? Caring? I get all that at Rotary." Dr. Willimon took the comment to heart, summing up the conversation with the professor with this question: "What makes the church, your congregation and mine, different, utterly essential, without equal, unique?" Willimon then ventured a response: "A congregation is Christian to the degree that it is confronted by and attempts to form its life in response to the Word of God."[4] He said that as Christians we are people of a book, the Bible. That does not mean that we either worship it, or claim that God is captured between its pages. It does mean that in our life with the Bible, we claim to have been confronted by the living Lord. That confrontation sounds to me like a very rich, very worthwhile conversation.

Welcome to this conversation with one particular portion of the Bible, Paul's Letter to the Romans. It's an honor to offer this reflection on Paul's letter. It is offered with fear and trembling, as the author wonders if he has either the capacity or the audacity to try to add anything to study of this complicated, mysterious letter, a work which has its own power and has had extraordinary impact on the history of the church. This reflection on this letter, an invitation to conversation with the text, is offered by a parish priest who has come to believe that vital congregations are actively engaged in conversation with Scripture, confronted by it as much as comforted by it. As we begin this conversation, know that we may raise as many questions as we answer. There will be occasions when we simply admit that we don't know what we don't know. The writing of this book has been undertaken with prayer that as readers in congregations work through this letter, the transforming power of God's grace will be experienced in their life with God and with each other.

## CHAPTER ONE

Welcome to the Conversation

God does not love us if we change. God loves us so that we can change.

—RICHARD ROHR, *BREATHING UNDER WATER:*
SPIRITUALITY AND THE TWELVE STEPS

I do not understand the mystery of grace—only that it meets us where we are and does not leave us where it found us.

—ANNIE LAMOTT, *TRAVELING MERCIES:*
SOME THOUGHTS ON FAITH

I appeal to you therefore, brothers and sisters, by the mercies of God, to present your bodies as a living sacrifice, holy and acceptable to God, which is your spiritual worship. Do not be conformed to this world, but be transformed by the renewing of your minds, so that you may discern what is the will of God—what is good and acceptable and perfect.

—ROMANS 12:1–2

Give us such an awareness of your mercies that with truly thankful hearts we may show forth your praise, not only with our lips, but in our lives.

—GENERAL THANKSGIVING IN THE DAILY OFFICE,
BOOK OF COMMON PRAYER

How is it that we change? How is it that we grow? Or to use the language of St. Paul, who wrote a letter to "all God's beloved in Rome," how can we be transformed? Think about your own spiritual journey, about moments when you experienced change, growth, transformation, or renewal. What contributed to those experiences? What got in the way?

Think about the faith community to which you belong. Perhaps review in your mind those communities that have shaped you over the years. They may be communities in which you were profoundly formed. They may be communities you left, perhaps even fled. You may be in recovery from such places. Then ask the same kinds of questions. How do congregations change and grow? What brings about transformation? What brings about renewal and new life in communities of faith?

In the letter that Paul wrote to the Christians assembled in Rome, we get a case study in change, as he holds out the possibility of transformation for members of a congregation he had never met, an assembly meeting in the city at the center of the empire. He wrote with an invitation, perhaps even a challenge, to experience transformation. His Letter to the Romans, widely considered to be authentic in authorship, sets the stage for a long-anticipated visit he hopes to make as he moves westward in his mission.

In this letter, he builds a case that change and transformation are real possibilities, effected not so much by human intention or endeavor, but as a result of God's gracious activity in their lives. There is no doubt that this letter, across the generations, merits attention as an exploration of the transforming power of God's love. We enter into conversation with this letter in the hope, indeed the confidence, that transformation can still take place in our individual lives and in the lives of the communities to which we belong.

In the organization of the New Testament, the twenty-seven books that comprise the Christian Scriptures, we begin with the work of the evangelists: four gospels and the Acts of the Apostles. We then come to a series of letters attributed to Paul, written either to congregations or to individuals. The Letter to the Romans comes first in that collection.

Perhaps it was placed first in the canon simply because of its length. But perhaps there's more to it than that. It offers the longest presentation of Paul's theology, a defense of the faithfulness of God, fidelity to the promises God has made, an argument extended over eleven chapters (with a few Pauline detours), leading into a discussion of the ethical implications of this theology in five final chapters. In some respects, this letter becomes a lens through which the other letters can be read. From start to finish, the letter argues for the transforming power of the proclamation of God's grace. Paul knew that dynamic at work in his own life. While in this letter he cannot be accused of oversharing as far as his own spiritual autobiography is concerned, he nevertheless expresses confidence that this same power can unfold in the lives of the members of this community addressed in this letter. This power can change not only individuals, not only this congregation, but can change the world.

This Letter in the History of the Church

Any introduction to this letter must note its impact on the history of the church over the centuries, as this letter has had extraordinary influence at critical moments. Century after century, it has been a catalyst, active in the renewal and reformation of the church.

As described in his *Confessions*, Augustine's conversion came in the fourth century, a convergence of influences (as most conversion experiences are) when he recognized a need for personal transformation. Perhaps today we would say he hit bottom. A key catalyst for change had to do with his conversation with Scripture. Specifically, he was led to Paul's Letter to the Romans, the effect of his conversation with Scripture noted in *The Confessions*, written in 397:

> But when a profound reflection had, from the secret depths of my soul, drawn together and heaped all my misery from the secret depths of my heart, there arose a mighty storm, accompanied by as mighty a shower of tears. . . . I flung myself down, how, I know not, under a certain fig tree, giving free course to my tears and the streams of my eyes gushed out, an acceptable sacrifice unto Thee. And, not indeed in these words, but to this effect, spake I much unto Thee: But Thou, O Lord, how long? How long, Lord, wilt Thou be angry forever? . . . Why is there not this hour an end to my uncleanness? I was saying these things and weeping in the most bitter contrition of my heart, when, lo, I heard the voice as of a boy or a girl, I know not which, coming from a neighboring house, chanting and often repeating, *"Tolle lege! Tolle lege!"* (Latin—"Take up and read!"). . . . So quickly I returned to the place where Alypius was sitting, for there I had put down the volume of the apostles, when I rose thence. I grasped, opened, and in silence read that paragraph on which

my eyes first fell—"Not in rioting and drunkenness, not in chambering and wantonness, not in strife and envying; but put ye on the Lord Jesus Christ, and make not provision for the flesh, to fulfill the lusts thereof" (Rom. 13:13–14). No further would I read, nor did I need; for instantly, as the sentence ended, by a light, as it were, of security into my heart, all the gloom of doubt vanished away.[5]

Conversation with Scripture changed the course of Augustine's life. It led him to a theology that asserted that the grace and love of God redirects human affection. Augustine's theology in turn redirected the course of the church. His interpretation of Paul's letters continues to shape the church, for better or for worse. In some respects, we work hard to correct Augustinian interpretation, perhaps insightful for his time but difficult to translate to our own. Key themes expressed in the Letter to the Romans, themes like the need all people have for power beyond themselves to redirect misguided love, are at the heart of Augustine's theology. At a critical moment when the empire was crumbling and it was not clear how the church would move forward, Paul's letters, and especially the Letter to the Romans, served as transformative guide. It had to do with the embrace of grace. That is not the only time in the history of the church that this letter has had that effect.

In the early sixteenth century, the Letter to the Romans was key to the development of the theology of Martin Luther, a theology that emphasized the belief that right relationship with God comes through the unmerited grace of God, revealed in Jesus's death and resurrection. This theology galvanized political, social, and ecclesiastical forces to contribute to the energy of the Reformation. As often happens in moments of spiritual change or development, Scripture served as a catalyst, providing a way for social and cultural transformation to take place.

The Letter to the Romans was key. Luther writes:

I greatly longed to understand Paul's Epistle to the Romans, and nothing stood in the way but that one expression, "the righteousness of God," in chapter 1:17 because I took it to mean that righteousness whereby God is righteous and deals righteously in punishing the unrighteous. . . . At last, by the mercy of God, meditating night and day, I gave heed to the context of the words . . . and there I began to understand that the righteousness of God is that by which the right-eous lives by a gift of God, namely by faith. Here I felt that I was alto-gether born again and had entered paradise itself through open gates. The whole of Scripture took on a new meaning . . . and whereas before the "righteousness of God" had filled me with hate, now it became to me inexpressibly sweet in greater love. This passage of Paul became to me a gateway to paradise.[6]

As in the case of Augustine, Luther's interpretation of Paul's letter, transformative in his own day but now centuries old, needs to be interpreted for our own time. Along with other leaders in these times of reformation and revival in the church (William Tyndale, John Calvin, John Wesley), Luther entered into conversation with this New Testament letter, opening the door to change and transformation in their own contexts. The Letter to the Romans shifted their individual spiritual journeys, and by virtue of their positions of leadership, shifted the culture around them. It began with conversation with Scripture, which led to the embrace of grace.

Karl Barth published his commentary on Romans in the early twentieth century as the horrors of the First World War were shatter-ing optimism about humanity in Europe. Technology applied to warfare brought unprecedented horrific results. What would theolo-gians and interpreters of Scripture say in the face of such carnage? Where was God in this collective experience? How could the human condition be explained when the best that humanity had to offer led to this kind of conflagration? Barth spent ten years as a pastor (1911–1921), a tenure that had profound impact on his theology as "Barth's liberal assurances were initially undermined by his exposure to the Swiss social democratic movement. . . . The outbreak of the Great War further disillusioned him. . . . Most of his former teachers signed a declaration of support for the Kaiser." Barth described his experi-ence as follows: "An entire world of theological exegesis, ethics, dog-matics, and preaching, which up to that point I had accepted as basically credible, was thereby shaken to the foundations, and with it everything which flowed at that time from the pens of the German theologians."[7]

Barth returned to a conversation with Scripture, especially study-ing the Letter to the Romans in 1916, which resulted in his

This letter has conveyed transformative, perhaps even explosive, power over the course of the history of the church.

commentary, first published in 1919. That commentary offered a critique of the liberal theology of the previous generations, at a time when hard questions about the power of evil emerged from the trenches where so many young men died. Barth's commentary was described in graphic terms, as if a bomb had been detonated on the playground of the theologians of his day. As we will see in reflection on the first chapter of this letter, Paul speaks of the "power" of the gospel. In Greek, the word for power is *dunamis,* which provides the root for the word "dynamite." This letter has conveyed transformative, perhaps even explosive, power over the course of the history of the church.

Barth's reference to the shaking of the foundations (a lift from the book of Jeremiah) brings to mind a series of sermons by Paul Tillich, collected under the title of *The Shaking of the Foundations.*[8] One of those sermons, prompted by the Letter to the Romans, speaks of the transforming power of grace. It provides a powerful introduction to our reflection on this letter. Prompted by a verse in Romans 5, Tillich speaks about the interface of sin and grace:

> Grace strikes us when we are in great pain and restlessness. It strikes us when we walk through the dark valley of a meaningless and empty life. It strikes us when we feel that our separation is deeper than usual, because we have violated another life, a life which we loved, or from which we were estranged. It strikes us when our disgust for our own being, our indifference, our weakness, our hostility, and our lack of direction and composure have become intolerable to us. It strikes us when, year after year, the longed-for perfection of life does not appear, when the old compulsions reign within us as they have for decades, when despair destroys all joy and courage. Sometimes at that moment a wave of light breaks into our darkness, and it is as though a voice were saying: "You are accepted. You are accepted, accepted by that which is greater than you, and the name of which you do not know. Do not ask for the name now; perhaps you will find it later. Do not try to do anything now; perhaps later you will do much. Do not seek for anything; do not perform anything; do not intend anything. Simply accept the fact that you are accepted!" If that happens to us, we experience grace.[9]

As we enter into conversation with this letter, here's the question this book will seek to address: Does Paul's letter still have a transforming word for our day? What does it have to say to a church in need of renewal? Pollsters indicate disheartening shifts in religious affiliation in our culture. Traditions and institutions face new challenges, including the sense that they are obsolete or irrelevant. Division and partisanship between human communities (including and perhaps especially religious communities) seem to be on the rise, as the moral failures of religious leaders and institutions are on display for all the world to see, as people increasingly self-identify as spiritual not religious. Against that background Paul's letter bears a message that matters. It holds the promise of renewed spiritual vitality that can emerge when the grace of God is embraced and proclaimed, when confidence is placed in the reality of God's love that comes as free gift, and when that gift is viewed expansively, not as the possession or province of one particular group.

The expression of trust in God's grace, a theme of the Letter to the Romans, has the power to change individual lives. It also has the power to change communities, which is why it matters that we enter into this conversation. Such a conversation does not mean that we will like or understand everything in the letter. Paul wrote out of his own context, with its own limits. Augustine, Luther, and Barth each interpreted this letter for their time. Our time has its own character, context, and challenges. In the spirit of conversation, a word that suggests companionship on the journey, we hope that faithful attention to this ancient letter may open the door for new insights into the expansiveness of the grace of God. As we enter into this conversation, a few introductory comments are offered, setting this letter in the context of other letters attributed to Paul.

Paul's Letters: What They Have in Common, How They Differ

J. Christiaan Beker, in his study of Paul, spoke of both coherence and contingency in Paul's work.[10] Coherence reflects a continuity of structure and theme. Contingency suggests particular or occasional dimensions, reminders that these letters were written to specific congregations or people.

When we speak of coherence, in terms of structure, we note that the Letter to the Romans follows the pattern of a number of other letters attributed to Paul. It reflects the ways letters were structured in Paul's day. Paul's letters often begin with a greeting and an expression of thanksgiving for the community or individual being addressed (though the terse beginning of the Letter to the Galatians gives the reader a clue that Paul is not entirely happy with this crowd, and that the letter that follows will be sharp in tone).

Paul introduces himself, in the custom of letters of his day, and seeks to establish authority from the outset, eager to get readers to see why they should pay attention to what he has to say. Often in these introductions, Paul will weave prayers for these communities into his discussion, perhaps incorporating portions of liturgy, hymns, and early creedal formulations that may have been in use when members of the early church assembled. After these introductions, Paul often will turn to the theological question, describing who God is, and what God has done, especially as revealed in the death and resurrection of Jesus Christ.

Paul encountered the risen Christ on that Damascus Road, an event described numerous times in the Acts of the Apostles, as well as in several of his letters. It is interesting to note that Paul, unlike gospel writers, seems to have limited interest (or perhaps even awareness) of the events of Jesus's life prior to Holy Week. His main focus is on the last week of Jesus's life, on what those events in and around Jerusalem reveal about Jesus and about the one whom Jesus called Father, the one whose continuing presence is known through the Holy Spirit. Again and again, in a variety of ways, Paul returns to the theme of divine initiative in the reconciliation of relationship between God and humanity, a transforming dynamic seen throughout the Letter to the Romans. This dynamic, which is as much an event as it is a theological principle, can be described as grace.

Having reflected on who God is and what God has done, Paul in his letters will often shift, in one way or another, to what we call the "so-what" factor. As pastor, as coach, as model of discipleship, Paul encourages his readers to consider the practical implications of his theological insights. What difference does the theology make for their lives in the world? These are always good questions to ask. What will these congregations do in response to God's grace? As we hear the challenge in the Ash Wednesday liturgy, will they accept the grace of God in vain (2 Cor. 6:1)?

A persistent practical theme, woven throughout all of Paul's letters, addresses a challenge for these communities. How will they live in unity, as a reflection of the grace of God? What will their unity (or lack thereof) say to a world that is watching?

The ethical portions of Paul's letter can get quite practical, speaking about the ways that Christians are to live in the world, in the community of faith, in households, in the work place, as citizens. These passages, some of them presenting troublesome obstacles for modern readers, reflect the culture out of which Paul wrote. That is why our conversation with Scripture matters. In each generation, communities of faith are called to interpret Scripture with the courage to affirm what they believe and what they refuse to believe, the courage to pose questions that animate faith.

Many of Paul's letters conclude with greetings and instructions to members of these congregations, reminding the reader that these are specific communications to specific folks, communications bearing authority. One might wonder whether Paul could have imagined these letters being read thousands of years later, thousands of miles away. That specificity leads us to recognize the contingent dimension to each one of Paul's letters, a dimension that bears noting as we begin this conversation. These contingent elements account for differences in the letters. We see that dimension in this Letter to the Romans, written at the height of Paul's career (probably somewhere between 54 and 58 CE). As he writes, he has been at this entrepreneurial work for a bit of time. The letter conveys learning from that experience. He's been on the road for a number of years, pursuing his entrepreneurial missionary effort. The letter, though written to a community he did not establish, filled with people he did not know, has a distinctive dimension. The letter addresses a unique audience, particular concerns, and perhaps most important, a specific agenda on Paul's mind.

To get a handle on the contingent or specific intention in this letter, we might compare it to other letters. When Paul undertakes the

Corinthian correspondence, he addresses a community he founded, a community about which he cared deeply, a community he knew well, a community battling specific issues, maybe even a community slipping away from his authority in the glow of a more dynamic, eloquent leader. We can read both affection and exasperation in the Corinthian correspondence (presented as two letters in the New Testament canon, though perhaps an amalgam of three or more). Paul weighs in on controversies about sexual ethics, money, leadership, and religious rules. (Apparently, there is nothing new under the sun, as these are issues about which the church still argues.) He seems to know the controversies and the antagonists quite well.

When Paul writes to the Philippian congregation, it is clear he is enamored of this congregation and encouraged by their faith journey. He writes to this beloved church from an ancient Near Eastern prison, which must have been a fairly grim setting. Yet the overriding theme of the letter is one of joy, born of intimate familiarity with the congregants, born of deep and abiding affection for them, born of confidence in the God who guides and provides. He is able to talk about specific challenges going on in the congregation, including a fight between two members, hard as it may be for us to believe that arguments ever happen in church.

When we come to the Letter to the Romans, we get little of that specificity.

Perhaps because Paul did not know this congregation, because he had not yet visited them, he may be less able to address them with that sense of familiarity. But that is not to say that there aren't specific issues on Paul's mind. He has an agenda. As an expression of the broader theme of unity and solidarity in the body of Christ, Paul is concerned about a collection of money for the beleaguered Christians in Jerusalem. The letter comes as a kind of promotional piece, getting the Roman Christians ready to participate in a contribution to the fund that Paul was collecting for those who lived in Jerusalem. That offering of financial support had a sacramental dimension, an outward and visible symbol of the unity that Paul wished for the church, a sign to the world of the transformative power of the gospel.

Beyond this interest in collecting financial resources for Christian brothers and sisters in need, Paul hopes to make a good impression on this community so that he could use this assembly as a launching pad for ministry to the West. The hope for his ministry, indeed, his ambition is to move westward to Spain where he wishes to begin another church, out of a desire to work in places where others have not been, a desire to have freedom to shape these communities in the ways he feels called. Though someone else had founded the community at Rome, Paul hopes that this community will help him reach his Western goal. The lengthy presentation of his theology in this letter provides a way to build a foundation for the work that lies ahead.

Finally, he addresses in this letter the relationship between the Jewish and Gentile communities, living in tension within the Roman Christian assembly, a tension reflected on a more widespread level in the city of Rome, and across the empire. The city's minority Jewish population was under fire. They had been expelled by the emperor, as we read in a rather chilling throwaway line in the Corinthian correspondence in which Prisca and Aquila are cited as coming to Corinth because as Jews they had been forced to leave Rome. As James Carroll has demonstrated in his book *Constantine's Sword,*[11] the roots of anti-Semitism run deep in the history of Western culture. As Paul writes to the Romans, it seems that Jews had been allowed to come back to the city of Rome, and to the Christian congregation gathered there. Reading between the lines of the letter, especially in that distinct section identified as chapters 9–11, there are issues about the relationship between the Jewish and Gentile communities. Paul intimates that boasting was taking place, one group claiming superior spirituality to another group. This is yet another illustration (as if we needed it) that there is actually little that is new in the life of the church. That provides all the more reason for us to enter into conversation with this early letter. This concern about boasting will appear throughout the letter, a coherent theme in Paul's work. As we see how it is addressed from Paul's perspective, we can begin to shape a faithful response to the divisions in our communities in our own day.

Many Conversations at Once

The understanding of history is an uninterrupted conversation
between the wisdom of yesterday and the wisdom of tomorrow.

—KARL BARTH, PREFACE TO THE 1ST ED., *THE EPISTLE TO THE ROMANS*

With that as an introduction, welcome to this conversation with
Paul's Letter to the Romans. The fact is, there are many conversations going on at one time. First, as we read this letter, this is a conversation between Paul and a particular gathering of Christians. We
are reading someone else's mail, maybe engaging in holy eavesdropping on a letter written in another time and place. As students of
Scripture, we must acknowledge that there is
much about author and recipients of the letter
that we do not know. It's always wise to come to
Scripture in that spirit of humility.

We are reading someone
else's mail, maybe engaging
in holy eavesdropping on
a letter written in another
time and place.

This is a conversation that Paul has with imagined questioners. While history has only preserved
one side of this conversation, as we read, we imag-
ine the questions that prompt Paul to write what he does. Again and
again, in the style of diatribe, he poses questions that would ostensibly challenge his argument. Then he answers them. As we reflect on
this letter and interpret its meaning, we will explore what it might
have meant to those first-century Christians to be part of this conversation.

This is a conversation that Paul has with his own Scriptures. As
Paul makes his argument, he does so with repeated reference to the
Scriptures he knew. As we move through the letter, we will note the
ways that Paul has that conversation with Scripture, noting the
authority he grants to the Scriptures of his tradition. For the Jewish
community, references to passages from the Hebrew Scripture
would indicate that this letter is not simply a product of Paul's intel-
lect or imagination, impressive as those may have been. To people
who honored tradition, Paul demonstrates that what he proposes
has holy precedent.

This is a conversation that Paul has with his God, as he raises
deep and timeless questions about God's faithfulness. He seeks
understanding, for the sake of these Roman Christians, but also for

himself, about the mystery of God's activity in the world, the surprising, occasionally inscrutable ways that God acts.

This is a conversation that Paul has with himself. While we get little of the autobiographic information that comes, for instance, in the Letter to the Galatians (chapters 1 and 2) or the Letter to the Philippians (3:4–4:1), we do have moments in which Paul's own struggles come through loud and clear. He grapples with freedom and compulsion, with anguishing questions about why some people have faith and why others don't, and with the persistent human propensity toward boasting, so toxic for community life.

Finally, this is a conversation that Paul unwittingly has with us, as we "take and read" to discover what this letter means to us in our own day. As we listen in on the conversation between Paul and a community he had never visited, we find in the liveliness of Scripture that we enter into conversation with the letter. We find that many of the questions about the faithfulness of God, about the struggles and shortcomings we face in our inner being, about the mystery of who believes and who does not, about the ways we are called to live in the world, about the ways we can be transformed, all these questions can be asked these days. As Anglicans, we will enter into this conversation mindful not only of the authority of Scripture, but also the call to approach the theological enterprise (and we are all theologians) with reference not only to Scripture, but to tradition, reason, and experience.

There are many ways one could go about engaging in conversation with this letter. Because of the way the letter is written, our journey through this book will trace the argument that Paul offers, with commentary on the passages, and plenty of questions along the way. He is, in fact, building a case, marked by a few diversions and digressions, even detours, along the way. We may find the case compelling. We may find it confusing. It may trigger questions. It may make us mad. But for all kinds of reasons, it is well worth the conversation.

This book is offered in the hopes that congregations will read Paul's letter carefully and prayerfully, using these chapters as a guide for engagement, considering what the letter said to the people who first received it, and what it says to us. As you read each of the chapters in this book, be sure to read the correlating passages in Paul's letter first. Mark your questions as you read the Scripture. As this book serves as companion to this letter, and as you read Paul's letter, let Paul's letter read you as well. Be open to its power to transform, as Paul describes the mystery of the grace of God, which meets us where we are but loves us too much to leave us there.

Let the Conversation Begin

At the end of this book, the reader will find an invitation to enter into conversation with the passages that have been considered, with questions about how those ancient words apply today. These questions are intended for personal reflection. Perhaps it is your spiritual practice to keep a journal. You may want to jot down questions as you read the words of Paul, or respond to the questions asked at the end of the book. You may want to discuss them with others and form a small group to meet for discussion.

As we begin this conversation, and before we actually read and respond to portions of the letter, take time to consider the questions listed in the back of the book. They have to do with your own journey of faith, as a way to enter into the call to transformation being offered by Paul to this Roman congregation.

Finally, as you enter into conversation with this portion of Scripture, offer this prayer for your own appropriation of its message:

> Blessed Lord, who caused all holy Scriptures to be written for our learning: Grant us so to hear them, read, mark, learn, and inwardly digest them, that we may embrace and ever hold fast the blessed hope of everlasting life, which you have given us in our Savior Jesus Christ; who lives and reigns with you and the Holy Spirit, one God, for ever and ever. Amen.[12]

And note as this prayer indicates, and as Paul's letter repeats, that ultimately the gospel proclaimed in this letter is about hope.

 # How Paul Introduces His Letter
(Romans 1:1–17)

Where the faithfulness of God encounters the fidelity of [men], there is manifested His righteousness. There shall the righteous man live. This is the theme of the Epistle to the Romans.

—KARL BARTH, *THE EPISTLE TO THE ROMANS*[13]

The letters attributed to St. Paul in the New Testament come in great variety. Some are quite short. The Letter to Philemon is just twenty-one verses. Some are longer, like the letter considered in this book. Some are addressed to communities, some to individuals. Some letters reverberate with joy, like the Letter to the Philippians. Although Paul wrote it from a prison cell, Philippians seems to speak of rejoicing in every other sentence. Others strike a harsh, judgmental tone, like the Letter to the Galatians. Some, according to scholarly consensus, come directly from Paul's hand, or at least his dictation. Others were apparently crafted by people who followed Paul's teaching, perhaps as products of a school of disciples. But while we acknowledge a mosaic of thought and reflection, there is a coherence that helps us speak about Paul's writings as a body of work, coherence noted not only in the structure of the letters as discussed previously. There is also coherence in the themes that Paul addresses. These themes are set forth right at the outset, in the introduction to the letter found in the first seventeen verses of the first chapter.

How would the key themes in this letter be described? It has been said that the gospels were written to answer two questions: "Who is Jesus?" and "What does it mean to be one of his disciples?" Those who wish to enter into conversation with the Gospels might apply those two questions to any given passage. Those two questions can provide a helpful lens, a tool in scriptural exploration.

In many ways, Paul's letters tackle variations on those two questions. These letters explore two questions. The first question: How are we to understand the God known in the Hebrew Scriptures and revealed in the person of Jesus? The second question: What does it mean to be a disciple, or in Paul's vision, to be part of the body of Christ? Both these questions are addressed in the Letter to the Romans, approached through several interrelated themes. We begin with reflection on questions about God's nature and character.

The first question: How are we to understand the God known in the Hebrew Scriptures and revealed in the person of Jesus? The second question: What does it mean to be a disciple, or in Paul's vision, to be part of the body of Christ?

Again and again throughout the letters, Paul explores the theme of the faithfulness of God, the first of several themes to be noted. At times, it can seem in this letter as if God is on trial. Paul knows what people of faith have always understood, which is that the circumstances of life, what the Prayer Book identifies as the changes and chances of life, can trigger questions about God's sovereignty and goodness. Can both be affirmed? For many, such questioning presents an either/or situation. God is either in control, but not all that loving, or God is loving but not really in control. The existential questions which that tension poses surface throughout Scripture, from the very beginning with Adam's accusation of the Lord God in the garden when he blamed God, saying, "The woman you gave me made me eat of the forbidden fruit." It was apparently God's fault. We see the tension in Job's unanswered question about God's inexplicable action that led to his iconic suffering. In the Gospel of John, the tension prompts Lazarus's siblings to offer a heartfelt plea at the tomb when they meet Jesus: "If you had been here, my brother would not have died." Perhaps we see that tension in Jesus's own mournful cry from the cross, the echo of Psalm 22, where he asks the one he called "father" why he has been forsaken.

In our conversation with Scripture, this tension gets our attention. The circumstances of our lives and any cursory scan of the morning paper can cause us to inquire into the goodness and power of God. At certain moments, especially in this letter, the question of the faithfulness of God, the question of inexplicable suffering seems to drive the argument. Paul knew that struggle in his own life, as he occasionally seems to struggle in finding an answer to the timeless question of whether God is faithful to God's promises.

Paul, the preacher, does indeed have an answer to proclaim, pointing to a second key theme that he proclaims as good news, as gospel. It has to do with the triumph of God found in the transforming power of grace, the unconditional and expansive embrace of God that precedes human activity, exceeds human boundaries, and transcends human suffering. Paul experienced amazing grace in his own life. As his letters occasionally venture into spiritual autobiography, in any number of confessional moments, he describes his own struggles, and the ways that the grace of God met him. That experience was powerful for him, presented repeatedly as the Damascus Road conversion, an event so significant that the liturgical calendar grants that event its own feast day (January 25). It was such a powerful experience that he dedicated his life to sharing it with others, founding and forging communities where transforming grace would be experienced.

A third theme that emerges in his letters has to do with the way that the transforming grace gets expressed in human relationships, and especially in the church. That expression of grace prompts a call to Christian unity. That theme shows up in all of Paul's letters but seems especially prominent in this Letter to the Romans. Paul repeatedly warns against the toxicity of a spirit of boasting. He sees that human dynamic as an idolatrous disposition by which human beings put themselves in the place of God. That which has been created is put in the place of the creator. Paul's singular focus on the need for unity (not uniformity) in the Christian community shapes his ethic. He is willing to exhibit considerable flexibility about a variety of issues (dietary observance, religious ritual) for the sake of the edification of the church. As he says in the correspondence with the church in Corinth: "'All things are lawful' but not all things are beneficial" (1 Cor. 10:23). He talks about becoming all things to all people. In our culture, this statement would suggest a lack of conviction, or standing for nothing. For Paul, it was a call to a ministry of gracious flexibility, perhaps even holy inconsistency. It was a spirit of service and humility moving beyond inclusion to radical hospitality, out of the conviction that no issue should be allowed to divide the body of Christ. It was a call to honor the other, which now finds expression in the Baptismal Covenant with its call to respect the dignity of every human being. Paul knows well, perhaps from his own piety and religious experience, that the ego will do its best to assert its rights. That's a caution to anyone dedicating time to an in-depth examination of Scripture, as it seems that the ego is no more insidious and divisive than when expressed by religiously observant people.

Because of the nature of that divisiveness, Paul will return to the theme of righteousness. In our culture, in our history, that word has been used to suggest moral correctness. To quote scholar Karen Armstrong: "Religious people often prefer to be right rather than compassionate. Often, they don't want to give up their egotism. They want their religion to endorse their ego, their identity."[14] In Paul's vision, righteousness describes right relationship, not right behavior. Paul has noted the human tendency toward divisiveness, based on ego. He will note human limitation in overcoming the power of this dynamic, so he focuses on the righteousness of God, gracious divine activity whereby human beings are set in right relationship with God and each other. It comes as a gift, an act of grace that is not dependent on human doing but on God's divine intention.

The faithfulness of God, the grace of God, the unity of the community, and the righteousness of God: these themes are interwoven throughout Paul's letters.

The faithfulness of God, the grace of God, the unity of the community, and the righteousness of God: these themes are interwoven throughout Paul's letters. We find that they are most fully expounded here in the Letter to the Romans. That may be one of the reasons that this letter appears as the first in the body of Paul's work. It may well explain why this letter has had transformative impact on the church throughout the history of the church. As we begin reading our way through this letter, we can note in the first seventeen verses the ways that these themes are set forth, right up front, so we can't miss them.

Paul's Greeting (Romans 1:1–7)

We can tell a lot about the content of Paul's letters by looking at the way he starts them. Each of the letters contains a greeting of some sort, in keeping with the form of letters in his day. In the first seven verses of the Letter to the Romans, Paul's warm introduction to this congregation includes a description of himself as servant of Jesus Christ, called to be an apostle. In these first verses, he establishes the continuity of his message with the Hebrew Scriptures, appealing to those Scriptures to make his argument and to win a hearing from his audience, many of whom will be familiar with the passages he cites. Jewish members of the community would understand the significance of his reference to the "prophets in the holy Scriptures" as he embarks on this discussion about his own proclamation of the gospel concerning Jesus Christ, the Son of God, descended from David according to the flesh. Continuity between the covenants of Israel and the covenant revealed in the ministry of Jesus is established up front. From the beginning of this letter, we are pointed to God's transforming power which for St. Paul is revealed in the resurrection of Jesus. In the resurrection, Jesus, the descendant from David's line is declared to be the Son of God. We learn at the outset of the letter that the experience of resurrection and Paul's encounter with the risen Christ has established his authority as an apostle, commissioning Paul to bring about the "obedience of faith among all the Gentiles."

Paul as Servant

The first verses of this letter give glimpses into the ways that Paul understands his own ministry. First of all, he is a servant of Jesus Christ. In what sense does Paul see himself as a servant? The word can also be translated slave. In other places, Paul speaks of himself as a prisoner for Christ. These offer echoes of Hebrew Scriptures, evoking the ministry of the prophet Jeremiah who was appointed to be a prophet to the nations (Jer. 1:5), who made reference to his own compulsion to be a prophet, even when it got him in trouble. Paul may have been alluding to the prophet Amos who resisted the call but nevertheless heard God speak. In the Letter to the Galatians, a letter focused on the transforming freedom that comes with the gospel, Paul speaks of how that freedom actually leads to service. "For you were called to freedom, brothers and sisters; only do not use your freedom as an opportunity for self-indulgence, but through love become slaves to one another" (Gal. 5:13). This passage may well have prompted Augustine to note the paradox that in God's service is perfect freedom, language woven into our Prayer Book (see the Collect for Peace, p. 57). In chapter 9 of the first letter to the Corinthians, Paul speaks of how this call to proclaim, this ministry in line with the prophets of the Hebrew Scripture, is not a ministry that he chooses. He writes:

> If I proclaim the gospel, this gives me no ground for boasting, for an obligation is laid on me, and woe to me if I do not proclaim the gospel! For if I do this of my own will, I have a reward; but if not of my own will, I am entrusted with a commission. What then is my reward? Just this: that in my proclamation I may make the gospel free of charge, so as not to make full use of my rights in the gospel. For though I am free with respect to all, I have made myself a slave to all, so that I might win more of them. To the Jews I became as a Jew, in order to win Jews. To those under the law I became as one under the law (though I myself am not under the law) so that I might win those under the law. To those outside the law I became as one outside the law (though I am not free from God's law but am under Christ's law) so that I might win those outside the law. To the weak I became weak, so that I might win the weak. I have become all things to all people, so that I might by any means save some. (1 Cor. 9:16–22)

As we enter into conversation with this introductory section of the letter, we find at the outset that questions of freedom and service recur. They call us to consider our own vision of spiritual vocation. To what extent do we see ourselves as servants, or slaves, or prisoners? Are we free agents? Is free will overrated? We will find these kinds of questions returning often in this letter.

Paul as Apostle

Along with the theme of servanthood, the theme of apostleship persists in Paul's letters. The word literally means one who is sent, or one who is sent forth. Once more we hear echoes of the Hebrew Scriptures. Paul's sense of his own apostleship evokes the call to any number of characters who heard the call from God, and sometimes imagined it to be a wrong number, or reacted in fear, or tried to get someone else to do the job, people like Moses and Samuel, people who were not the most qualified like David or Solomon, people blatantly unqualified like Jacob. We are reminded of the prophet Isaiah who after a mysterious encounter with God's holy presence says those dangerous words: "Here am I, send me." In response, the Holy One tells him to go. We can hear echoes of the experience of the prophet Ezekiel who hears the divine voice saying: I am sending you to the people of Israel.

But there is more to the reference of apostleship than simply a call that comes to one who is sent to do God's work. In the political dynamics of the early church, the question of authority was closely tied to a claim of apostleship, a claim based on an encounter with the risen Lord. In other letters, Paul speaks of having been one who was "untimely born," that is, he did not have the opportunity to see Jesus prior to his death or in the forty days after his resurrection. He missed it by just a very short time. The experience of conversion on the Damascus Road, repeatedly recounted in the New Testament, constitutes for Paul the kind of authoritative sighting, the kind of commissioning that will lead people to listen to him. Again, as we enter into conversation with this letter, we might begin this reflection with inquiry into our own sense of call, our own sense of being sent into the world. In what sense do we see ourselves as apostles? And where do we find authority?

In his introduction, Paul claims that his servanthood and his apostleship come from the God who has been active over generations, highlighting a continuity with the Hebrew Scriptures that will prove to be an important theme throughout the letter, as Paul argues that God has been faithful to the promises God has made. The covenant relationship established between God and humanity has not been abrogated. For Anglicans, who note the power of the tradition in theological reflection, Paul provides a model for how to address the challenging questions of our lives by conversation with ancient texts, by conversation with tradition.

On the basis of his apostolic authority, Paul addresses this congregation with introductory comments that not only provide insights into the way Paul regards his own vocation. These comments also offer insight into his regard for the recipients of this letter, this Roman congregation. With warmth and cordiality, he refers to them as God's beloved, called to be saints, each in their own way set apart for a work of witness in the world. Pause and consider what association you have with the word "saint"? Who do you know who fits that bill?

For Paul, all the members of the community are saints, not in the technical sense of a term that evolved in the medieval church, a term that suggests spiritual superheroes. Rather, sainthood suggests God's prior activity, God setting apart this community, a community of people who have been called to belong to Jesus Christ and will be given their own mission in the world. With that spirit of vocation for a community formed by God's gracious action and God's gracious call, Paul bids them grace and peace, not from himself but from "God our Father and from the Lord Jesus Christ." He invites these early Christians into conversation, in ways that both challenge and invite them to be part of a transformed community and to experience transformation in their individual spiritual journeys. As we read this letter, Paul will invite us as well into that kind of conversation in ways that may well transform us as we consider what it means in our world to embrace grace.

Thanksgiving and Prayer for This Community (Romans 1:8–15)

After offering a greeting, Paul proceeds to offer thanks to God for a community whose members he never met, a common practice in letters of the day (though notably absent from the Letter to the Galatians). Paul offers thanksgiving because the faith of this community has been shared throughout the world. To those words of thanksgiving, he adds an expression of his desire to visit them, to impart some spiritual gift for their strengthening, pointing to the occasional character of this letter. He expresses his desire to be encouraged by them, presumably with a gift of financial support, "reaping the harvest" among them as he has from other Gentile communities, ostensibly for the sake of those in need in Jerusalem. Again, that gift, coming from newly formed Christian assemblies that had sprung up around the Mediterranean rim, had a sacramental dimension. The expression of mutual support represented, in a most tangible way, the unity of the church, the body of Christ, gathering to address common need. Paul in his introduction alludes to what we might call a spirituality of fundraising, saying right up front that the offer of material support, the use of financial resources for the sake of those in need, was a deeply spiritual enterprise. Such generosity was an act of worship signifying the union of the church, which again is a prime concern for the apostle. In our own conversation with these Scriptures, in our own time when our global village makes us keenly aware of the needs of God's children around the world, this witness to the unity of the church expressed in a spirit of generosity challenges us to service around the world.

Paul concludes this opening section by declaring eagerness to come to Rome, to proclaim the gospel to them, to share with them this good news which he believes has transformative power for the lives of individuals, for the lives of the Christian community, and ultimately for all people. With that in mind, he offers a succinct statement of his mission, his purpose, his vision in verses 16 and 17 of this first chapter. He tells his readers that the gospel has this transforming potential, that really religious people and really irreligious people are being brought together under God's power. In this event, the theme of grace is determinative, not human religious observance. Paul recognizes, perhaps the preacher preaching to himself, that human pride kicks in all the time, especially when it comes to piety and religious practices. He has come to learn, perhaps the hard way, that all people stand in need of divine intervention, divine initiative to move forward in the face of that power which is greater than power of our own. We need help. In the midst of our own brokenness, our powerlessness, God works, revealing the power of God's gracious spirit. The next two verses express, with clarity, that hopeful vision.

The Thesis of the Letter (Romans 1:16–17)

> For I am not ashamed of the gospel: it is the power of God for salvation to everyone who has faith, to the Jew first and also to the Greek. For in it the righteousness of God is revealed through faith for faith, as it is written "The one who is righteous will live by faith."

Pause as you are reading and consider the words that give this thesis statement its shape. Ask yourself about your own association with words like "gospel" and "salvation." What do you understand by the words "righteousness" and "righteous"? What kind of faith do you think is being discussed here? What kind of power is Paul talking about?

For I am not ashamed of the gospel: it is the power of God for salvation to everyone who has faith, to the Jew first and also to the Greek. For in it the righteousness of God is revealed through faith for faith, as it is written "The one who is righteous will live by faith."

These two verses function as the thesis for the letter. For all the complexity of the argument that will be developed in chapters that follow, the great themes of this letter are represented in two short verses. If the letter were a symphony, with various movements and interweaving themes, these two verses function as an overture, giving the reader an idea of what they are about to hear. Key words and major themes, artfully and succinctly presented, serve as a mission statement, perhaps even an elevator speech. Paul tells the Romans what he's going to tell them, identifying themes to be unpacked at length in the following pages. For that reason, these two verses merit attention, with reflection on key words that signal persistent themes throughout the book.

Not Ashamed: Paul affirms that he is not ashamed of the gospel, a phrase with significance because it stands in contrast to what Paul will say later in the letter when he describes the spiritual dangers of boasting. He decries boasting, that egocentric dynamic which tears the fabric of the community, creating divisions between groups within the church, between those who are in the church and those who are outside the church, between those who are new to the church and those who have been part of the community for some time, and between those who disagree on issues of belief and practice. In this letter as in others, Paul insists that there is no cause for boasting, except in the gift of God's grace. Ephesians 2:8–10 (another brief passage that sums up an entire letter) explicitly strikes that theme. It says that by grace we are saved, though not because of works lest anyone should boast. It's not hard to imagine that Paul had to wrestle with his own ego. His compulsive work ethic, creative energy, superior intelligence, and fine upbringing would make it easy to set himself above others. Perhaps the preacher is preaching to himself when he warns against boasting, or at least identifies the right kind of boasting. In the opening of this letter, he indicates that he is not ashamed. Said another way, he is willing to boast in the power of God's righteousness.

The Gospel: Paul is not ashamed of this gospel. The word "gospel" in the Greek is *euagellion,* from which we get terms like "evangelist" and "evangelical." In contemporary American culture, those words carry baggage. Like many of the words bandied about by church folk, its meaning and power need to be reclaimed. It means good news, and who doesn't need to hear good news? We hear an echo of the Hebrew Scripture in this word, evoking passages from Isaiah (Isa. 52:7, a passage cited by Paul in chapter 10 of this letter) that speak of the beauty of the messenger who brings good news. The term *euagellion* also had a secular sense, conveying the image of a ruler, with the suggestion of a triumphant proclamation, a recognition of God's activity. That notion of triumph suggests the power that Paul describes next in this mission statement.

Power: In his commentary, Anders Nygren wrote: "The gospel is not the presentation of an idea, but the operation of a power. When the gospel is preached, it is not merely an utterance, it is something that occurs . . . snatching them from the powers of destruction and transferring them into the new age of life."[15] As Paul Tillich said: "Accepting God's grace is the ultimate event of faith. Grace changes everything."[16] The word in Greek is *dunamis,* from which we get the word "dynamic" and even "dynamite." Paul proclaims a message that has the power to transform. It has even on occasion acted explosively, with the power to shatter old ways of thinking. We see its dynamic effect in the vision of the Christian community expressed by Paul in Galatians 3, where in Christ there is neither male nor female, slave nor free, Jew nor Greek. We see it in the imagery of the Letter to the Ephesians, which speaks in chapter 2 about a dividing

Eschatological: An orientation toward the future focused on the end times, the last days, marked by intimations of both hope and judgment.

wall being torn down, no longer dividing Jew and Gentile. That vision of a community transformed by grace is one that the church has never been fully able to live into.

Salvation: The good news of this power that Paul proclaims is that it will effect salvation, another word that is loaded, as if salvation were equated with a ticket of admission, or a source of differentiation between those who are in and those who are out. The word for "salvation" in Greek is *soterian.* It suggests wholeness, healing, wellness. Rather than a status, it is an indication of a process initiated by God. With an eschatological dimension, it expresses hope (Rom. 13:11), the "eventual safe passage through human trials and divine judgment to eternal bliss."[17] If we look for echoes of the Hebrew Scriptures in this passage, we might be led to Psalm 98:3: "He [God] has remembered his steadfast love and faithfulness to the house of Israel. All the ends of the earth have seen the victory of our God." Similarly, in several passages in Isaiah, we read of the ways in which the Lord will reveal his holy arm before all the Gentiles, so that all the corners of the earth will see the salvation that is with God (Isa. 52:10).[18]

Everyone Who Has Faith, Jew and Greek: Paul, a fierce partisan for much of his life, driven by a clear sense of the boundaries of the community, offers a case study in how the gospel can transform relationships. He articulates and advocates a dynamic gospel with the power to transform communities in such a way that they will be inclusive of Jew and Greek, transcending boundaries that had kept those two communities apart. Such an expansive vision of God's activity makes a claim that we tend to resist: the notion that all will be included in God's saving power. That radical vision of universal inclusion is a theme that will come at the climax of the letter at the end of the eleventh chapter.

The Righteousness of God: The entire letter circles around the theme of the righteousness (in the Greek, *dikaiosyne*) of God as revealed to humanity. An alternative translation for the word might be the justice of God. After this introductory section, Paul describes the righteousness of God in terms of impartiality (we're all in this together) in chapters 1:18–3:20. In the next section, chapter 3:21–8:39, Paul describes the righteousness of God in terms of God's right-wising or justifying action. In chapters 9–11, God's righteousness is described in terms of God's faithfulness to promises made, balancing a tension between God's promises and apparent human rejection of those promises. The final section of the book (chapters 12–16) shows how the righteousness of God gets reflected in human relationships, the ethical piece. In Paul's vision, this righteousness is understood as God's activity, not human activity. This attribute is not a matter of human doing. It's not about morality, about people doing the right thing, or being right, which is how we often perceive religion. This righteousness, understood as God's activity, is primarily a relational term. God's righteousness is that quality that reaches out to human-ity and sets people in right relationship with God, when that rela-tionship has been broken and when the power to reconcile is beyond human capability

Revealed: In the Greek, the word is *apokaluptetai,* from which we get the English word "apocalypse." In common usage, the word "apocalypse" suggests terrifying destruction, the end-times. Think Hollywood special effects. Certainly, many of the apocalyptic pas-sages of Scripture, from Ezekiel to Daniel, from the Gospel of Mark to the Revelation of John include violent imagery evoking fear. But there is another, less terrifying but no less powerful sense of the word, one that can be associated with the righteousness of God. It suggests unveiling, as if the curtain on a stage is being drawn back to reveal dramatic action.

In Paul's letter to the Corinthians, he speaks of seeing through a glass dimly, but then seeing face-to-face. What is being revealed? The mystery, that secret will be presented in a most focused way in chap-ters 9–11. In this letter, and specifically in those particularly mysteri-ous three chapters, the revelation that will unfold has to do with God's activity, the righteousness of God, which brings about com-munity and is inclusive of all. Echoes of the Hebrew Scriptures can be heard as we refer to Psalm 98:2 ("The LORD has made known his vic-tory; he has revealed his vindication in the sight of the nations") or Isaiah 51:4–5 ("Listen to me, my people and give heed to me, my nation, for a teaching will go out from me, and my justice for a light to the peoples. I will bring near my deliverance swiftly, my salvation has gone out and my arms will rule the peoples; the coastlands wait for me, and for my arm they hope"). The theme of revelation is indispensable, signaling that the faith to which we are called is really about our perception of God's loving intention, about our receptivity to that intention born of absolute dependence on God who has been, is now, and will be faithful.

Through Faith, for Faith: There are a number of ways to translate this rich and enigmatic phrase that, if nothing else, will prompt lively conversation. What do we mean by faith? Is it our work? Is it God's work? This phrase may mean, for instance, beginning and ending in faith, a way to emphasize the importance of faith. It may mean gift and response, suggesting that synergy of God's initiative, God's overture to humanity met with the human response of love, gratitude, and obedience. A third possibility might be that God's righteousness is revealed out of the faith of Jesus and leads to the faith of his followers (i.e., through the faith of Jesus for the faith of his followers). When Paul concludes with the reference to Habakkuk, which says that the righteous shall live by faith, he may well be talking about the righteousness of Jesus who in his death and resurrection conveys the power to change us all. Again, we have a foretaste of the discussion to come, not only in this letter (especially with reference to Abraham in chapter 4), but in the history of the church where the persistent question of the relationship between God's activity and human response has been discussed over the centuries. Paul affirms in his thesis statement that the power of this gospel, now being revealed, will unfold in faith, a reflection of the faith, or perhaps the faithfulness of God. It calls us at the outset of the letter to consider the mysterious synergy of human response to God's activity, a tension explored in the New Testament and in the history of Christian theology in the discussion of grace and works.

The Righteous Shall Live by Faith: As punctuation to this mission statement, Paul turns to the Hebrew Scripture (Hab. 2:4), a passage that draws attention to this prophet of the fifth century who explored the issue of the faithfulness of God. The prophetic ministry of Habakkuk addressed the issue of theodicy, as the faithful commu-

nity waited with patience for the appearance of
God's justice at a time when there seemed to be little hope. (It is from the book of Habakkuk that
we get the language of the great Advent hymn,
"Watchmen, tell us of the night," people scanning
the horizon for that place where God's justice

Theodicy: The defense of
God's goodness and power
in light of the existence of
evil and suffering.

might appear.[19]) This quote about the righteous living by faith also
suggests the faith of Abraham, a character who appears prominently
in this letter in chapter 4, and will show up in other letters attributed
to Paul and in other portions of the New Testament. Abraham serves
as an example of God's righteousness acting in and through human
agency. Again, it is up for discussion whether the faith referred to in
this last phrase is the faithfulness of God, or the faithful response of
human beings. Paul crafts this phrase in such a way that it might well
be both, and in that way, may sum up this letter.

This first chapter has devoted attention to these opening verses
because they set the tone for all that follows. Having set forth his thesis, having articulated his mission statement, having offered the overture, in the next section, Paul launches into a discussion of the
challenges that face all of humanity.

What's the Problem?
(Romans 1:18–3:20)

If only it were all so simple! If only there were evil people somewhere insidiously committing evil deeds, and it were necessary only to separate them from the rest of us and destroy them. But the line dividing good and evil cuts through the heart of every human being. And who is willing to destroy a piece of his own heart?

—ALEKSANDR SOLZHENITSYN, *THE GULAG ARCHIPELAGO,* 1918–1956

A friend and parishioner came to a commitment to the Christian faith as an adult. After years of fervent agnosticism, he described the gradual process that led to newfound faith, the way in which the faith came to make sense to him, the way his faith came to life. A clever man, a graduate of an Ivy League university with a major in philosophy and much brighter than his parish priest, he told me that he had arrived at a place where he could sum up his faith in his own variation on the title of a popular book. He said he had come to understand the gospel this way: "I'm not okay. You're not okay. But that's okay."

As his pastor, I was not entirely comfortable with his summation. Like any self-respecting Episcopalian, I wanted to add nuance, to say "Yes, but it's more complicated than that." I was eager to unpack his understanding, making sure that he had considered the power of original

Original Sin: A doctrine developed over the centuries that unites all humanity in separation from God. How that condition has been transmitted, genetically or otherwise, has been variously interpreted and a source of theological dispute.

blessing, the goodness of creation. But I had to agree with him that evidence of flawed human condition was irrefutable.

G. K. Chesterton noted that while certain theologians dispute original sin, it was "the only part of Christian theology which can really be proved."[20] One only had to look as far as the morning news, or for that matter, the local church, to see evidence. I appreciated that my friend had put his finger on an essential truth, one reflected in this second section of Paul's Letter to the Romans.

This section of the Letter to the Romans offers insight into how Paul understands the challenge facing all of humanity. If we imagine someone asking him: "Paul, what's the problem?" this next section suggests his answer. As will be true throughout this book, a conversation with this passage will hopefully trigger questions about our own spiritual lives, and about the lives of faith communities in which we participate. Is there any need for change and transformation, or are we content with our spiritual lives? Are we doing and being all we are called to do and be? Are we living in right relationship with God and neighbor? Do we fall short? If we do fall short, how do we understand the gap between where we are and where we want to be? How might we close the gap, as individuals, as faith communities?

After Paul introduced himself to this congregation in his greeting, establishing his authority to write to them, asking for a hearing and for hospitality when he visits, after he told them what he planned to tell them in the succinct thesis statement in Romans 1:16–17, he begins to build a case for the transforming power of the gospel, the righteousness of God evoking a human response of faith. In order to make the case, he needs to explain why any transformation is needed. He knows well what many people participating in organized religion have come to understand, which is that human beings, and especially religious human beings, are change averse. He will point to the truth of the core of his thesis (i.e., that the power of the gospel is the revelation of the righteousness of God) by presenting its antithesis (the revelation of the wrath of God). In his mind, both of these revelations occur not at some future date, but are unfolding in the present time.

So where is it that Paul sees the wrath of God revealed, and what is the nature of that divine attribute? In verse 18, on the heels of his thesis statement, Paul dives in to the discussion, using provocative language to get the attention of his readers, alerting them to the urgency of the need for transformation in their individual lives and in their community, a need that they hold in common, whether they are religiously observant or not. He describes a universal condition, or more to the point, a universal predicament forged by common dependence on God's mercy to overcome the ways that humanity has fallen short, and has experienced broken relationship between God and neighbor. The salvation mentioned in the thesis statement will be a healing of those broken relationships, a move toward wholeness.

Paul's argument brings to mind the teaching of Jesus in the beatitudes, at the beginning of the Sermon on the Mount in Matthew 5. That familiar list of blessings begins with the statement most familiarly stated as follows: "Blessed are the poor in spirit." The New Revised English Bible artfully translates that first beatitude this way: "Blessed are those who know their need of God." As Paul presents his vision of the solidarity of the human condition, he sums it up by saying, in this passage and in subsequent chapters, that all people, without exception, stand in need of God's mercy. Blessing will come to those who know that need. Indeed, blessing cannot come apart from recognition of that need. That common need, not doctrinal uniformity or orthodoxy, not common ancestry, not fulfillment of an ethical code, will provide the basis for the unity of the church. It will take a transformation of the heart.

In order to establish this vision of human solidarity, Paul must paint a picture of how broken the relationships have become. Perhaps for dramatic effect, he will get everyone's attention by talking about how the wrath of God is revealed against those whose sins seem particularly egregious and notorious.

The Wrath of God Revealed against Bad People Out There . . . (Romans 1:18–32)

So how do we hear that phrase, "the wrath of God"? Gary Larson, the cartoonist, often wanders into theological conversation with his humor. In one of his cartoons, he depicts God, an old man with long white beard, sitting at a computer. On the screen, there is a picture of a grand piano. The rope lifting it into an apartment window has snapped. The piano is in free-fall, about to crush an unsuspecting pedestrian. God sits at the keyboard and is poised to press the "Smite" button. Imagery like this may come to mind as we move into this next section that speaks of the wrath of God. In our conversation with Scripture, early on in the letter, we are asked to inquire into the meaning and relevance of such language.

With a provocative introduction of the wrath of God, Paul has moved our conversation with Scripture into challenging territory, calling us to wrestle with the text, determining what we believe in light of the texts and also what we refuse to believe. Quickly, we are presented with questions not only about the character of human behavior but also about the character of the God of the Bible, the character of the God we worship. How do we speak about the wrath of a loving God? Are wrath and love incompatible? Does discussion of the wrath of God belong to another age marked by more primitive theologies? Isn't Paul, isn't Jesus, isn't the New Testament all about love and grace?

A discussion of wrathful divine judgment triggers comments about the ways that people have entered into conversation with the Scriptures. An impression is often shared from the pulpit, through the lectionary, in scriptural interpretation, in our church classes and Sunday schools, that the God of the Hebrew Scripture somehow had a personality shift by the time the New Testament rolled around. In this unhelpful caricature, which has—by the way—done little to help Jewish-Christian dialogue, the God of the Hebrew Scriptures is characterized by wrath, anger, fear, and judgment, a God who is all about the rules, God hurling lightning bolts, God pressing the "smite" button. The God of the New Testament is, on the other hand, characterized by love and kindness. That impression might well be dispelled with some of the parables of judgment taught by Jesus, with his clearing of the temple, and in the letter before us, with the abrupt way Paul launches into this section focused on the revelation of the wrath of God.

In our own conversation with Scripture, how are we to describe this attribute of God, which seems so jarring after Paul's warm introduction to this Roman congregation? Paul has heralded a gospel that reveals the righteousness of God. How does he come so quickly to speak of wrath? Centuries after the letter was written, we consider what Paul means by that phrase, how it has anything to do with good news, and how it has anything to do with us. Is the wrath of God an emotion, a psychological attitude of God? Does the God of the Bible stand in need of anger management? Is the wrath of God simply an objective description of a state of estrangement and alienation, an impersonal force triggered in opposition to evil? Is it a dynamic that, in turn, triggers automatic moral degradation among people, switching on automatically, almost like a thermostat?[21] Is it an active response from a God who demands loyalty, love, and worship? Is it a passive, divine response to human choice, God allowing people to be what they choose to be? Is it a symbol for the retribution that comes to humans because of a willful turning away from God? Is it a matter of God simply allowing human beings to stew in their own juices?[22] Are there any answers that will put such questions to rest? This is one of those places where our conversation with Scripture may feel more like wrestling with Scripture.

Paul argues that the wrath of God comes as a response to the sin of idolatry, a variation of the sin of boasting which we have already noted as one of the persistent themes in this and other letters. That sin is a refusal to give glory to God, a refusal that is insidious because it tells a lie. As part of his argument that this dynamic is widespread, indeed universal, Paul indicates that there is no excuse for those who commit this sin of idolatry and trigger the revelation of God's wrath. There is no excuse for failing to worship God. What can be known of God is evident to all. The truth that God is distinct from humankind is there for all to see. In an apparent expression of natural theology, Paul says that that truth about God is irrefutably apparent in creation. All humanity, whether they've heard the news taught or proclaimed, can recognize that there must be something more, something above and beyond, something greater. All who fail to acknowledge, all who fail to worship come under the wrath of God, as relationship with God is broken and as God hands people over to idolatrous tendencies.

God Gave Them Up (Romans 1:24, 26, 28)

While we might struggle to make sense of the wrath of God, we get clues into Paul's vision when he speaks of divine wrath as a process by which people are being handed over (1:24, 26, 28), *paradoken* in the Greek. Paul notes that human beings, human communities have sunk into depravity, a result of human action and human faithlessness. A break in relationship with God, the failure to worship God, results in a break in relationship with other human beings. One of the earliest examples of this in the biblical record would be the first murder, in which Cain kills his brother Abel in what is apparently a dispute over proper worship. One could say that this is the first recorded church fight. A misguided relationship with God on the part of Cain redounds to a broken relationship with his brother. At heart, the activity that causes this break in relationship, an activity that might safely be described as depraved, can be characterized as idolatry, exchanging the glory of the immortal God for images resembling a mortal human being or birds or four-footed animals or reptiles.

Throughout the biblical record, idolatry seems to be the central temptation that comes to human beings. We see it in the story of Adam and Eve in the garden, eating forbidden fruit so that they would become gods. We see it in the story of the Hebrews wandering in the wilderness worshipping a golden calf when it seemed that God had abandoned them, as the leader appointed by God (Moses) lingered on the mountaintop, as the people lost confidence in the God who had led them so far, and had instructed them to make no graven image. We see it in the story of Israelites demanding a political ruler, a king, believing that they knew better than God how to organize their common life. Because of the disorder that comes from this misplaced affection, three times Paul says that God "gave them up," resulting in increasing levels of depravity. That action on God's part suggests that the wrath of God has that quality of people falling into the consequences of their own actions. For an audience that included readers steeped in the Jewish tradition, Paul's description of idolatry in his letter echoes descriptions that surfaced in writings from Hellenistic Judaism. The following passages from the Wisdom of

Solomon demonstrate how the creation of idols leads to the corruption of life, another way of explaining the wrath of God:

> For while they live among his works, they keep searching and they trust in what they see, because the things that are seen are beautiful. Yet again, not even they are to be excused for if they had the power to know so much that they could investigate the world, how did they fail to find sooner the Lord of these things. But miserable, with their hopes set on dead things, are those who give the name "gods" to the works of human hands. . . . For the idea of making idols was the beginning of fornication, and the invention of them was the corruption of life (Wisdom 13:7–10, 14:12)

"Miserable, with their hopes set on dead things." That is certainly one powerful way to describe the effects of the wrath of God.

How Do We Enter into Conversation with Difficult Texts (Romans 1:2–27)?

A wise pastor concluded a training of Sunday school teachers with this challenge. He said: "Be mindful of the Hippocratic oath: Do no harm." It was striking to the teachers, who came to see that when they were teaching the Bible, inviting young people into conversation with Scripture, they were dealing with a powerful resource. It mattered how they taught these stories. With that in mind, we consider the ways that we hear, read, learn, mark, and inwardly digest these passages, in light of recent discussions in the church about human sexuality.

As Paul describes the wrath of God, a response to the idolatry that led God to hand them over to increasing levels of depravity, we pause to consider several verses in this first chapter that represent specific challenges for contemporary conversations in the church. They have to do with the subject of human sexuality. They represent one of the few places that Paul addresses the subject. Our conversation with Scripture invites us to ask how sexuality was regarded in Paul's day, how it is regarded in our own, and how we deal with the differences in those perspectives.

We recognize that Scripture bears its own power, especially evident in modern expressions of Christianity, where there are a variety of views about the authority of Scripture and many ways to read and interpret Scripture. In the history of the church, a number of passages have been used in discussion of social and political issues, and specifically in the church's deliberation around issues of justice. Scripture, over the years, has been used to justify slavery, as well as to promote the case argued by the abolitionists. Scripture has been used to bar women from leadership roles in churches, and it has been used in support of the ordination of women. Shakespeare was on to something when he said "Even the devil can quote scripture." (For an interesting study of these varied approaches, get a copy of *The Bible Tells Me So. The Uses and Abuses of Scripture.*[23]) A number of passages from Paul's letters have been used in these kinds of debates about social issues. In recent times, several passages from Paul's letters have been isolated in the church's discernment about human sexuality, and cited as authoritative.

In many of our lectionaries, when these early passages from the Letter to the Romans appear in the schedule, verses 26 and 27 are omitted. These two verses make reference to sexual activity of women considered to be unnatural, and to men who are consumed with passion for other men. In the cultural context in which Paul wrote, they characterize sexual relations between members of the same sex as examples of depravity at its most extreme. In these verses, set in the context of a longer diatribe where Paul is working the crowd into a frenzy, Paul condemns these relationships as an expression of idolatry and a refusal to give glory to God. There are several texts in the Hebrew Scripture which seem to assert that such sexual relations are forbidden. Today, in various cultures around the world, various societal and religious norms continue to make that case, at great cost to those of same-sex orientation.

As we read this letter in our contemporary context, and seek to hear what the Spirit is saying through these texts, we recognize the ways that these few verses have been used and abused in contemporary conversation within the church about homosexuality. How we read and apply these texts matters, for it is not simply reflection on documents from another time. They speak to our own day. In the church, across denominations, these verses have been among the most quoted of Paul by those who oppose inclusion of homosexual persons in the life of the church, who would seek to bar them from ordained ministry, or deny marriage between persons of the same gender.

It is certainly difficult to know what Paul had in mind when he spoke of these relationships. Many commentators have concluded that he was speaking of something entirely different than what we know in our own time to be committed same-sex relationships marked by mutuality and fidelity, relationships for which the church has now developed liturgies of blessing. As modern readers of these texts, who engage with these texts out of the confidence that they continue to speak to us, we are challenged to find a meaning for our own time. The questions that we ask of Scripture include these two. First, what does it say for the people for whom it was written? And second, what does it say to our own day? The answers to those questions may not be the same.

We acknowledge that we may not actually know what Paul was referring to when he spoke about those relationships. We may not know what those kinds of relationships meant to the people of his day. Whatever Paul had in mind, he disapproves, and sees the activity as a sign, a symptom of broken relationship with God.

Then we must also ask what it means to our own day, and note among other factors, rapidly shifting understanding about the nature of human sexuality, and specifically homosexuality. We note also the ways that our culture has evolved in its discussion about all kinds of social issues (slavery, gender, warfare, use of money) for which there are biblical texts that may be used to support one point of view or another. We are called as people of faith, to see these Scriptures in the context of our own tradition that derives ethical and theological perspectives by synthesizing Scripture, tradition, reason, and experience.

Scholars have written volumes about these passages. Interested readers can find a great deal written about how homosexuality was viewed in Paul's time, and how it is being understood in our time. These verses, again sometimes left out of lectionaries and so left out of the conversation in our churches, invite us to think about how we read Scripture. In our conversation with Scripture we are left with several choices: We can dismiss all of Scripture as too bound to its cultural setting to have meaning for our time. We can work hard to make passages from another cultural context apply to our own time. We can do the work of balancing Scripture, tradition, reason, and experience to forge a faithful understanding that the Scriptures with which we converse, the Scriptures with which we often wrestle, are products of human beings, shaped by cultural norms of the time. We can read Scripture through the lens of Paul's ethic, expressed again and again, that what is most important is that which builds up the body of Christ. What is most important is the expression of love.

> We can read Scripture through the lens of Paul's ethic, expressed again and again, that what is most important is that which builds up the body of Christ. What is most important is the expression of love.

With that in mind, we are called to repent of the ways that these and other texts have been lifted from biblical and cultural context to be used to exclude and injure homosexual persons. (They are sometimes referred to as clobber texts.) That kind of exclusion flies in the face of the wideness of God's mercy that will be a key theme of this letter. It breaks the baptismal promise to work for justice and peace and to respect the dignity of every human being.

These verses remind us that conversation with Scripture is often a struggle. We may not always like or understand what we read. We may not know what the author had in mind. We may find that the ethical predisposition of the biblical author differs from our own. We may conclude that a faithful reading of the text causes us to part company with the literal meaning or traditional interpretations of the text. It may provide an opportunity to note the ways we have grown and learned over the years, to recognize that we must continue to grow and to learn. We may be called to focus not only on what we believe but also on what we refuse to believe. For this author, Paul's condemnation of sexual activity in these two verses must be read in their context. They cannot be used to exclude or oppress those in our culture whose identity includes same-sex orientation. The verses must be subjugated to a higher ethic, which is the expression of love as the greatest of spiritual gifts, and as the witness of the community to the world.

Above all, it seems we are called to see these verses in the context of Paul's argument. One of the important ways to wrestle with the text is to make note of a rather unfortunate chapter break. The first chapter should not be read separately from the second. As we move into that second chapter, the argument continues. Using his considerable rhetorical skill in this diatribe, which may actually be a version of such arguments familiar to his audience, Paul drives his readers to note those people out there who have broken God's law and are worthy of God's wrath. This is in many ways a setup. We only get half the story if we do not notice how all people, including those who condemn the depravity that Paul has depicted with such fervor (including Paul himself), are drawn into the common need for God's grace and mercy.

Those Bad People Out There Are No Different than Us (Romans 2:1–16)

Like a politician playing to his base, in the previous verses Paul has roused the faithful, getting them worked up in righteous indignation about all those bad people out there. Paul may have been using literary forms familiar to his audience. When the crescendo of excoriation reaches fever pitch, he artfully turns the tables on his audience. He has been talking about bad people out there. He has been talking about "them." Now he speaks directly to his readers and says: "You are not all that different from those folks. You are doing the same things as those bad people." Throughout the history of interpretation of the Scripture, people have often stopped at the end of chapter 1, and have missed the central point of this section. Paul levels equal judgment against those who pass judgment. (One might imagine the preacher is preaching to himself.)

Paul tells his readers: when you pass judgment on others, you are condemning yourself. His language is reminiscent of Jesus's teaching in the Sermon on the Mount when he says, "Do not judge, so that you may not be judged. For with the judgment you make you will be judged" (Matt. 7:1–2). The main point is this: Paul says that the wrath of God is being revealed not only toward those whose lifestyle is offensive to the religiously observant, and so are regarded as depraved. He also says that the wrath of God is being revealed against those who judge others for the kinds of depravity he has listed not only in this passage, but in other letters as well. That act of judgment is in fact just another version of idolatry, a matter of putting oneself in the place of God as judge.

One can imagine that those who hear the letter saying something like this: "What are you talking about? We've never done those horrible things!" Paul might answer by pointing to the teaching in the Sermon on the Mount in which Jesus talks to his disciples about the law that forbids murder. One can imagine his disciples saying: "Of course, we would not commit murder." Then Jesus says that if you harbor ill thoughts toward a neighbor, it's as bad as killing that person. It comes from the same place. Paul may have in mind passages where Jesus speaks of adultery, and says that if you look after a woman with lust in your heart, you have committed adultery with that woman. The consequences may not be the same. The disposition of the heart may well be. All people are to be held accountable before God for their works. In a variety of ways in this letter, Paul makes the point that all people fall short. We are in this together.

It's worth noting the desire to make a tidy package of Paul's theology and to say that it's all about grace and not about works. In these verses (Rom. 2:6–11), Paul seems to indicate that human activity matters. He writes that "there will be anguish and distress for everyone who does evil . . . but glory and honor and peace for everyone who does good." It sounds like Paul is saying that human activity, accomplishment, or achievement will determine salvation. Taken in the fuller context of all of Paul's writing, we conclude that this is not so much an expression of works righteousness as it is an effort to note that all have fallen short of the glory of God. The anguish and distress comes to all, another way of describing the wrath of God that is meted out to Jew and Gentile, another way of noting the solidarity in the human condition. We are all in this together, "for God shows no partiality" (Rom. 2:11).

Does Religious Observance Get You Off the Hook? (Romans 2:17–29)

As the argument continues, the focus is sharpened. Paul turns to those in the congregation who are addressed as Jews, a crowd he knows well, a crowd in which he sees himself. Echoing language that Jesus used in countering opponents, Paul challenges members of the community who are claiming to be guides to the blind, light to those in darkness, correctors of the foolish, teacher of children.

Again and again, Paul claims that what matters is the disposition of the heart. Said another way, it is a matter of worship. Addressing the Jewish community, in an audacious way, he interprets the distinctive mark of the community, the covenant expressed in circumcision by saying that if one breaks the law, circumcision has become uncircumcision. He claims that those who may not have gone through the physical act of circumcision may know more about walking in the way of God than those who fulfill the outward requirements of the law. Again, in a provocative style that will recur in the letter, Paul chooses to reinterpret what it means to be a Jew and what it means to be in right relationship with God.

As we read this letter, we are cautioned as those outside the contemporary Jewish community against trying to define what it means to be a Jew. The circumstances in which Paul raised this issue are different than our own. Our conversation with a passage like this calls us to recognize the history in which the church has failed in honoring the Jewish community. Here, Paul, himself a Jewish person, says that outsiders may see more clearly than those who have traditionally claimed to understand the law. His provocative talk leads him to recognize that he is walking a fine line in this discussion, perhaps at risk of abrogating the covenant that God had made as described in the Hebrew Scriptures. That would be an untenable conclusion if indeed the letter is meant to argue for God's faithfulness to God's promises. So he dials it back a bit as his argument continues in affirmation of God's faithfulness to the covenant.

God's Faithfulness to Covenant
(Romans 3:1–9)

Paul claims that the unfaithfulness of human activity can be seen not only in the depravity of those people out there, but in the shortcomings of the most religious, those close to the core of the community. But none of that abrogates God's faithfulness to the promise. As we have said, and as we will continue to discover, this letter is a defense of the integrity of God in a world where things may have seemed to have spun out of control, even divine control. (That sense is not limited to the first century. A quick glance at the morning news might help us realize this is still a relevant concern.)

Paul knows the questions he will be asked, questions to be explored in the next section. Specifically, he anticipates the question about what it means to be justified. Asked another way, how can human beings be brought into right relationship with God? Paul concludes with one of the great themes of the book in verse 9: "We have already charged that all, both Jews and Greeks, are under the power of sin." As we saw in the thesis of the letter, which speaks about the power of God's righteousness, and as we will see later in the letter, Paul sees all human beings under the sway of powers greater than human will or intention. The notion of human free agency is over-rated in Paul's mind. In order to make the argument that all of humanity exists under the sway of these powers, Paul will return to conversation with the Scriptures he knew (Rom. 3:10–18), offering a series of quotations that underscore his main point: there is no one who is righteous.

All of Humanity Subject to God's Judgment (Romans 3:10–20)

In this passage, we realize why it can be challenging to enter into conversation with Scripture attributed to Paul. At the beginning of the third chapter, he has indicated that the Jew has an advantage, "much in every way." That advantage comes as they were entrusted with the oracles of God. Even if those oracles were not embraced by those to whom they were delivered, they nevertheless indicate a sign of God's commitment and God's faithfulness. Paul then balances that affirmation with another point of view, which is to ask: Are we (assuming he puts himself in the company of the Jews in his audience) any better off than others? In Romans 3:9, he says definitively, no, we are not better off. All people, both Jews and Greeks, are under the power of sin.

All people, both Jews and Greeks, are under the power of sin.

To confirm that point to his Jewish audience, he strings together a series of texts taken mostly from the Psalms as well as other sources in the Hebrew Scriptures. We are once again reminded that this conversation with Scripture is not only with the Letter to the Romans. As Paul quotes the Hebrew Scriptures fifty-seven times in this letter, it becomes a conversation with all of Scripture.

Paul speaks to his audience that would include Jews familiar with these Scriptures. He may have assembled these verses himself, or borrowed from someone else's work. Either way, he claims that these texts confirm his point that there is no one who is righteous, no one who has understanding, no one who seeks God. That is nothing new. They've heard this before. They should not be surprised that the whole world may be held accountable, that the whole world has fallen short of the glory of God. If there is any hope for humanity it will not come through human striving, which even at its most fervent and rigorous falls short and thus becomes its own kind of idolatry. The hope is that the righteousness of God will indeed be revealed (will be apocalypsed) with dynamic, transforming energy. In that revelation, the faithfulness of God will be revealed as well, as grace is embraced.

Paul then introduces a discussion about the law, a word that appears in many of his letters, with various meanings depending on the Greek word used, and depending on the context. In Paul's mind, the law bears its own revelatory power. It reveals the limits of human possibility. On the one hand, it is useful in the way it holds everyone accountable. Yet the law is not sufficient to protect human beings from the egocentrism that puts humanity at the center, not able to move them into right relationship with God and neighbor. We'll explore the revelation of that right relationship in the next section of the letter.

## CHAPTER FOUR

# Christ Addresses the Human Condition
(Romans 3:21–4:25)

O to grace how great a debtor daily
I'm constrained to be. Let thy goodness
like a fetter bind my wandering heart
to thee. Prone to wander, Lord I feel it.
Prone to leave the God I love. Here's my
heart, o take and seal it. Seal it for thy
courts above.[24]

We're all in this together. Paul, in the previous section, has asserted that we all have experienced broken relationships with God and neighbor. How will reconciliation, healing, salvation, wholeness emerge? Paul has made the point that all humanity comes under the judgment of the wrath of God. Everyone has missed the mark, without exception. In the mystery of faith, those who imagine that they have not missed the mark may have missed it by the widest margin. For this latter group, the ego easily takes over and as one friend has stated, ego is really an acronym for "edging God out." So if that is the good news, I suspect we'd hate to hear the bad news. Paul sees the good news, the gospel revealed in the death and resurrection of Jesus Christ.

We have heard little from Paul about his understanding of Christ since he opened the letter introducing himself as a servant of Christ. In that introduction, Paul affirms that the resurrection event presents Christ as Son of God. But in the section we just read, in which he has analyzed the human condition, he said little about Jesus. Paul has indicated the ways in which human beings have fallen short. But that's not the end of the story. In the remaining portions of chapter 3 and in chapter 4, he presents a hopeful vision, made possible because of the transformative gospel that he is not ashamed to proclaim. He claims that the revelation of God's righteousness, God's justice, will unfold so that all those under the power of sin may find freedom. That liberation comes with the death and resurrection of Jesus Christ, the divine response to the bleak assessment of the human condition that Paul has presented.

But Now (Romans 3:21–31)

How can one speak of good news after what we've just heard of Paul's description of the human condition? Here the theme of disclosure or unveiling becomes important, as Paul describes the revelation of the righteousness of God. A new reality is introduced with these two important words: "But now." What exactly has happened now?

Paul says that the righteousness of God has been revealed, countering the revelation of the wrath of God about which we've been hearing. In Paul's mind the revelation of the righteousness of God is a decisive, objective event, historically rooted in the experience of Jesus. The event is not dependent on human response, lending it an unconditional quality. In Christ, Paul describes a new situation, noted by Ernst Käsemaan as not only the logical antithesis of what has gone before, but as an eschatological turning point, a temporal matter as much as it is a shift in argument. Käsemann sees God's saving action "extended towards a world which barricades itself against God's intervention."[25] This justice, this revelation of righteousness (or right relationship) is not a static moral quality, but rather a dynamic moment revealed through faith in Jesus Christ. It has not only become visible. It is now being made public, now being proclaimed.

It is indeed God's saving action, God's intervention, met with the response of human faith. As we noted in the references to the thesis statement that spoke about faith, the phrase "through faith" can be translated in a number of ways, all of which has generated discussion about how we understand faith. We might conclude that faith itself is a human work, so that all who believe would create a separate category of people, establishing some kind of human distinction. But that's not the only way to think about it. Faith can be described as God's work in terms of the faith of Jesus Christ, by which the faithfulness of God is expressed in the faithfulness of Jesus.

This is a repeated theme in Paul's letters. Philippians 2:8 speaks of the mind that was in Christ Jesus who "humbled himself and became obedient to the point of death—even death on a cross." Romans 5:19 (to be discussed in the next chapter) compares Adam and Christ: "For just as by the one man's disobedience the many were made sinners, so by the one man's obedience the many will be made righteous." In chapter 6:1–23, Paul will talk about how those who trust in God are justified. Throughout this letter, there is synergy, a cooperative effort begun with God's initiative and received in human embrace. Belief, as a matter of the heart, is the result of God's mysterious working in and through the human will. To fail to trust in this way is, to repeat Käsemann's phrase, to barricade oneself against God's intervention, perhaps another way of describing the experience of the wrath of God.

In Romans 1:18–3:20, the universal fallen condition (i.e., falling short of the glory of God) is affirmed. But now, in this section, Paul notes the universality of gift (Rom. 3: 22, 23), accessible to those who believe, the power of grace with expansive and ultimately universal effect. Paul notes once again that there is no distinction. The only way out of the existential predicament he has described in the opening chapters is through the gift of grace. In a way, this passage (and specifically Rom. 3:21–26) gets to the heart of Paul's argument. The good news is expressed in Romans 3:24: "They are now justified by [God's] grace as a gift, through the redemption that is in Christ Jesus."

After the bleak assessment of the human condition that claims that all have fallen short of the glory of God, is there hope for any of us? Is there good news? Paul affirms the gospel of Christ, powerfully revealing the righteousness of God, available to all, who in Christ are able to share in the glory of God that had been lost. It has to do with grace, the result of activity on God's part that provides the basis for the unity of the church. The hope that Christ holds out is the creation of a community of faith in which there is no distinction. That new community is manifested in the radical vision of Galatians 3:28–29: "There is no longer Jew or Greek, there is no longer slave or free, there is no longer male and female; for all of you are one in Christ Jesus. And if you belong to Christ, then you are Abraham's offspring, heirs according to the promise." We see it in the image of dividing walls being broken down in the letter to the Ephesians (Eph. 2:14–22) that speaks about the creation of one new humanity. We see it in the familiar imagery about love being the greatest gift in 1 Corinthians 13, a passage that has little to do with weddings but has everything to do with the idea that the church, the body of Christ, will be united, again one of the great concerns that Paul has for the congregations he pastors. The vision of that new community is Paul's hope for the ever-expanding collection of congregations around the empire who will remain connected and support each other, with prayer and financial resources as outward signs of the reality of the risen Christ. As such, our conversation with this letter continues to be about Paul's understanding of Jesus.

Who Is Jesus for Paul?

Who do you say that I am? That is the question Jesus asked his disciples at a pivotal moment in the journey to Jerusalem. It is a question all disciples must ask. It is certainly a question that came to Paul in his own journey of faith. In his other letters, specifically in 1 Corinthians 15:1–11, Paul makes the point that he did not have the opportunity to meet Jesus in the flesh. Comparing himself to other apostles who directly encountered Jesus, he describes himself as one who was untimely born. He is the least of the apostles, not only because he participated in persecution of the first Christians, but also because he did not meet Jesus in person. Nevertheless, he says that by the "grace of God I am what I am."

In his writing, there are examples of passages that provide strong echoes of Jesus's teaching. The ethical passages at the end of the Letter to the Romans evoke the Sermon on the Mount with the call to love enemies. Several passages in Paul's letters specifically quote Jesus, most notably the passage in 1 Corinthians 11 that describes the institution of the Eucharist, language woven into the liturgy of the

Book of Common Prayer. But Paul's interest in Jesus has little to do with the circumstances of his birth. He has limited interested in the teaching of Jesus. If Paul knew about the miracles of healing and provision and deliverance, he doesn't mention them in the letters. In the same way that the gospels do not function as biography but instead devote most attention to the last week of Jesus's life, for Paul the meaning of Jesus is revealed in the events of Holy Week and Easter. The story of Jesus's death and resurrection, the power those relatively recent events had, mark the turning of the ages, unleashing the power of the gospel to transform, a power that Paul described as turning his own life around, transforming the communities where it is embraced.

A Few More Key Words to Consider

In this important section of Paul's letter, Paul introduces a few more key concepts which give insight into the ways that Paul answered Jesus's question: Who do you say that I am?

Grace: Jesus is, for Paul, the one who has come to bring about transformation, to deliver all of humanity from its solidarity in separation from God, described by the fact that all have sinned and fallen short of the glory of God (3:23). He says that that separation from God, that distance, that gap has been bridged by grace, as a gift. This gives opportunity to focus on the theme of grace in Paul's theology. While not explicitly expressed in the thesis statement of Romans 1:16–17, the theme of grace undergirds the righteousness of God as transforming power, accessible to all, which comes not in response to human accomplishment or distinction, but as gift. Pause in your reading and think about the word "grace" and its call for reclamation in our culture, where it is often used to signify an aesthetic sense. Its deeper sense suggests love freely and lavishly given, without condition, providing a way to move forward.

Law: Jesus is the one who reveals a new understanding of the law. Paul navigates complicated territory here, arguing at once for continuity and discontinuity between the community of his heritage and the new community created by the proclamation of the gospel. He is led to interpret the role of the law, beginning and ending this section with a discussion of the ways in which the law is to be properly

Atonement: Reconciliation between God and humanity, often involving repentance and reparation.

understood. The righteousness of God is manifested or revealed not through the law, although the law and the prophets attest to it. The law is not sent as a "summons to achievement."[26] Instead, the kind of faith that Paul describes gives back to law its character as promise, putting an end to pious achievement, and witnessing to salvation. It is easy to caricature law as simply a series of rules. For Paul, the picture is more complex, deeper, and more powerful as the law points toward the new community of grace.

Sacrifice: Jesus is portrayed by Paul as an atoning sacrifice by his blood, effective through faith. Various atonement theories about how sacrifice takes effect have emerged throughout the history of the church, some promoting images of a violent God, wittingly or unwittingly encouraging similar human behavior. As Paul makes reference to sacrifice in Romans 3:25, he may be having his own conversation with Scripture, echoing passages like Leviticus 16, which details the annual sanctuary purification rite (which in our time provides the antecedents for the observance of Yom Kippur) in which the effects of sin were liturgically resolved. He may have had in mind images of the Suffering Servant presented in Isaiah 53, among other places in Second Isaiah, which describes the self-offering of the Messiah and in the Christian tradition, prefigures the passion of Jesus. Paul may have had in mind the narrative of 4 Maccabees 17:22, in which the power of this sacrifice counters the cruel tyranny of Antiochus: "Through the blood of those devout ones and their death as an atoning sacrifice, divine Providence preserved Israel that previously had been mistreated."

Second Isaiah: Scholars detect several voices gathered into one book attributed to the prophet Isaiah in the Bible. These several voices reflect different historical circumstances and different theological perspectives, and so are referred to as First, Second or Third Isaiah.)

Whatever the case, this understanding of atonement has roots deep in the Hebrew Scripture and its historical context. It does not seem that Paul has developed an extensive theory here. Over the history of the church, varied theories about atonement stand as a dividing line among Christians. Some are passed down from cultural contexts that no longer make sense to us. In Paul's mind, the death of

Jesus was not a mechanical offering but the faithful death of a living human being. It was an act of obedience, an act "through faith" (3:25). On the cross, Jesus relinquished any claim to life or worth apart from God's gift. Thus he is the righteous one by faith, and thus he lives by virtue of resurrection.[27] As this word is introduced here in the letter, we are mindful that it surfaces again in chapter 12 where Paul invites the faithful to be living sacrifices, a force for edification, and not destruction or violence.

Justification: Finally, Jesus is the one who opens the pathway for justification. If you were to ask what the Letter to the Romans is about, in many quarters you may get the answer: justification by faith. What does it mean to be justified?

It's easy to imagine justification as a human activity, as in: "I am justified in doing such and such." Paul's vision comes at it another way, as the emphasis here is on what God has done in Christ, not the human activity of an expression of faith. In the death and resurrection of Jesus Christ, power has shifted in such a way that God justifies the one who has faith in Jesus. Is it a legal fiction, God pretending? Is Paul talking about making faith a work? When Paul speaks of justification by faith, is he making it a human activity? To make righteous, to justify, is not about virtue. The emphasis here is on what God has done, not the human activity of an expression of faith. In Paul's mind, that justification has come through the offering of Jesus.

Then What? (Romans 3:27–31)

Paul seems to realize that he has stirred it up a bit. In the spirit of the lively conversation he is having with this congregation, Paul anticipates a string of questions. He goes ahead and answers them. Here are some of the questions: What happens to our boasting? It is excluded. On what premise is it excluded? On the principle of faith, not works. Is God only the God of the Jews? Do we overthrow the law? No, we uphold it (at least when properly understood).

In Paul's mind, faith and law support each other. Faith in Christ does not overthrow the law. It confirms it and helps it achieve its result.[28] The purpose of the law is that sin might be unmasked (perhaps revealed or disclosed), so that human beings might be brought to consciousness of it, so that they might be brought to realize their absolute dependence on grace. Paul seems particularly interested in unmasking sin, not as morality, but as a power. The law demonstrates that sin rules with limitless sway.[29]

Paul recognizes that he is walking a fine line here, as he needs to affirm his own Jewish tradition while welcoming those outside his tradition. With that in mind, Paul returns to a theme that he has already addressed and that will come up again, the theme of boasting. In God's economy, there is no basis for distinction. Grace functions simultaneously as judgment, as it sets the religious person in company with the godless. Faith and boasting are incompatible. Indeed, faith puts an end to boasting, since faith is about what God does, not about the human ego or effort, not about one group set above another. All of this is not an abrogation of the law. Quite the contrary, it is the fulfillment of the law, reminiscent of Jesus's vision of the law in the Gospel of Matthew: "I have come not to abolish [the law] but to fulfill [it]" (Matt. 5:17). It is also accessible to all. To illustrate this theme, Paul turns to the story of Abraham.

Why Abraham? (Romans 4:1–25)

In chapter 3, Paul has been exploring questions of grace and law, sacrifice and justification. How do these concepts fit in with his tradition? How do they point to the faithfulness of God?

As Paul builds the case for the wideness of God's mercy extending beyond boundaries that previously divided religious communities, he continues the conversation with the Scriptures of his tradition. In fact, at this point and at others, he brings his own interpretation of those Scriptures to the service of his argument. That is something we all do, as we consider our own interpretations of the meaning of Scripture, and our conversations with sacred text.

As he reflects on his tradition, Paul has opened himself to charges that he is abandoning that tradition, anticipating the question of whether he is overthrowing the law by his emphasis on faith. He says (3:31) that he is not overthrowing the law, but rather he is upholding it, arguing (as many reformers do) that he is actually preserving the tradition. While it might appear to some that he is doing away with his tradition, inventing something new and discontinuous, he claims he is not surrendering the privileges that have come to his people.

Rather, he is finding new meaning for those privileges, for the law. That new meaning is rooted in promise, a reinterpretation, perhaps a revisioning of the tradition that will allow the tradition to move forward into the future. In order for that to happen, the law must be properly understood. No shrinking violet, Paul seems confident that he is the one capable of describing that new vision.

It may not be hard to imagine why it might have made some angry. It is no wonder he got in trouble. To counter his critics, Paul is eager to show continuity with the teaching of the Hebrew Scripture. He appeals to Abraham, the revered father of the race (Isa. 51:1f), described in the portion of the Mishnah pertaining to marriage, the Kiddushin (iv.14). In that passage, Abraham is noted as one who "performed the whole law before it was given, for it is written, 'Because that Abraham obeyed my voice and kept my charge, my commandments, my statutes, and my laws.'" Abraham is described in the portion of the Mishnah pertaining to sayings of ancient fathers, the Aboth (v. 3) as an icon of absolute trust and fidelity: "With ten temptations as Abraham our father was tempted, and he stood steadfast in them all." The religion of the Hellenist synagogues saw Abraham as the fulfillment of Greek virtues (Philo, Abraham, 52ff, Josephus, Antiquities 1. 256).[30]

Paul had many characters from the Hebrew Scriptures to choose from in bolstering his argument. He could have cited Moses or Elijah, representatives of the law and the prophets, two characters who for the early church clearly sum up the narrative of the Hebrew Scriptures—witness their presence at the transfiguration as told in the synoptic gospels. He could have told the story of David, the great king of Israel, or shared the narrative of prophets like Isaiah and Jeremiah, with whom Paul seems to identify as he proclaims his apostolic message. He will talk in short order about Adam, but will not cite him as model, example, or test case. He chooses instead to draw on the example of Abraham, the patriarch of Judaism, Christianity, and Islam to establish that the tradition is indeed established on the principle of faith and not on adherence to law. Pause before you read further and consider what you know about Abraham. His story is told in the book of Genesis, chapters 12–25. Ask yourself why Abraham would have been chosen.

Paul speaks of Abraham as an ancestor according to the flesh in an appeal to a Jewish audience. But Abraham is chosen not only because of his role as father of the faith. His story begins with Abraham living outside of the land of Israel, being called for no reason indicative of special merit. Abraham follows, moving forward, "not knowing where he was going" (Heb. 11:8). He is regarded as the first proselyte, and emerges as the father of proselytes. In Genesis 23:4, he is referred to as a stranger and a sojourner, so Abraham can be seen as father of believing Gentiles as well, not on the grounds of the covenant of circumcision but on the grounds of faith. Abraham's story indicates that the God of the Jews is also the God of the Gentiles. He is thereby uniquely situated in the narrative of the Hebrew Scriptures as the person who bridges this gap. As such, he serves Paul's argument well.

In order to expand on Abraham's role, consider these key points. First, Abraham was deemed to be righteous (i.e., set in right relationship to God) in Genesis 15:6, well before he was circumcised, as described in Genesis 17:11. The notion that Abraham could live in holy and whole relationship with God before the law, before the covenant of circumcision was given, establishes in and through the tradition that God is able to be in relationship with human beings above and beyond the legal tradition, above and beyond particular religious tradition, a radical thought. Abraham was declared righteous not because of his fulfillment of the law, but because of his faith.

Second, we encounter in this passage the idea expressed in Genesis 15:6 that faith was reckoned to Abraham as righteousness, so that God was the one who made it happen. Paul claims that the one who graciously intervened to bring about righteousness for Abraham is indeed the same divine power working in this Roman congregation.

Paul furthermore says that the role of the law was not to make people righteous (Rom. 4:13–15). Paul links Abraham's leap, his trust, his absolute dependence with the faith of his audience. Though it looked like there was no future (which could have been the conclusion that readers got from the first section of the gospel), with both Abraham and Sarah too old to have children, Abraham had faith in the God "who gives life to the dead and calls into existence the things that do not exist" (4:17). A similar idea is expressed in 1 Corinthians by Paul (1:28), but also echoes the power of the resurrection that

Paul says is the occasion for the revelation of this powerful, dynamic, transformative gospel. Abraham is distinguished not as adherent to the law, but as one who embraced the promise. Paul argues that God is still faithful to those promises, and that they are now being fulfilled in the death and resurrection of Jesus.

What Other New Testament Passages Say about Abraham

In our conversation with Scripture we note how various writers of the New Testament regarded Abraham, indicating the ways that Paul and other early Christian writers were in conversation with the Scripture of their tradition. In addition to his appeal to Abraham in the Letter to the Romans as that unique figure who represents Jewish and Gentile tradition with the promise of blessing for all, Paul refers to Abraham in the Letter to the Galatians. In that letter, which is different in tone from the Letter to the Romans, Paul writes to a church (or churches) that he believed had abandoned the gospel he had preached. In the Letter to the Romans, Paul introduces these people to the gospel of grace. In the Letter to the Galatians, Paul calls this community back to the promise they had abandoned, the gift of grace. Our intention here is not to dive deep into the Letter to the Galatians, but to notice how Paul regards Abraham, the one to whom faith was reckoned as righteousness, or right relationship with God, the one who offers blessing not only to Jews but to Gentiles.

Paul commends those who accept this promise as gift, and do not see it as a reward for works, which would set up human distinction, lead to boasting, divide the community, and invalidate the gift of the cross. Paul also in this letter notes the significance that the promise that came to Abraham preceded the giving of the law, indeed, even preceded the covenant of circumcision:

> Just as Abraham "believed God, and it was reckoned to him as righteousness," so, you see, those who believe are the descendants of Abraham. And the scripture, foreseeing that God would justify the Gentiles by faith, declared the gospel beforehand to Abraham, saying, "All the Gentiles shall be blessed in you." For this reason, those who believe are blessed with Abraham who believed. For all who rely on the works of the law are under a curse; for it is written, "Cursed is everyone who does

not observe and obey all the things written in the book of the law." Now it is evident that no one is justified before God by the law; for "The one who is righteous will live by faith." But the law does not rest on faith; on the contrary, "Whoever does the works of the law will live by them." Christ redeemed us from the curse of the law by becoming a curse for us—for it is written, "Cursed is everyone who hangs on a tree"—in order that in Christ Jesus the blessing of Abraham might come to the Gentiles, so that we might receive the promise of the Spirit through faith. Brothers and sisters, I give an example from daily life: once a person's will has been ratified, no one adds to it or annuls it. Now the promises were made to Abraham and to his offspring; it does not say, "And to offsprings," as of many; but it says, "And to your offspring," that is, to one person, who is Christ. My point is this: the law, which came four hundred and thirty years later, does not annul a covenant previously ratified by God, so as to nullify the promise. For if the inheritance comes from the law, it no longer comes from the promise; but God granted it to Abraham through the promise. (Gal. 3:6–18)

Later in the New Testament, the author of the Epistle to the Hebrews crafts a letter that is really a sermon, an encouragement, an exhortation, offered to Christians caught in the crucible of persecution. They are eager to know how to move forward into an uncertain future. In the eleventh chapter, the author offers a survey of characters in the Hebrew Scripture, people who demonstrate what it means to have faith, that spirit of trust or absolute dependence. The author includes Abraham in the review of that great cloud of witnesses. Indeed, Abraham gets a lot of airtime in this section, again with a focus on the promise he embraced, moving forward in a leap of faith, as what Kierkegaard called the knight of faith, setting out for a place that he was to receive as an inheritance, not knowing where he was going. As suggested in the readings from Romans, there are references to the power of resurrection implied here. Abraham and Sarah have a child, even though they were too old. (Therefore from one person, and this one as good as dead, descendants were born, "as many as the stars of heaven and as the innumerable grains of sand by the seashore" [Heb. 11:12].) In the passage that follows, see how they are both commended for their faithfulness as outsiders, strangers, and foreigners on earth, those seeking a homeland, desiring a better country, filled with promise:

By faith Abraham obeyed when he was called to set out for a place that he was to receive as an inheritance; and he set out, not knowing where he was going. By faith he stayed for a time in the land he had been promised, as in a foreign land, living in tents, as did Isaac and Jacob, who were heirs with him of the same promise. For he looked forward to the city that has foundations, whose architect and builder is God. By faith he received power of procreation, even though he was too old— and Sarah herself was barren—because he considered him faithful who had promised. Therefore from one person, and this one as good as dead, descendants were born, "as many as the stars of heaven and as the innumerable grains of sand by the seashore." All of these died in faith without having received the promises, but from a distance they saw and greeted them. They confessed that they were strangers and foreigners on the earth, for people who speak in this way make it clear that they are seeking a homeland. If they had been thinking of the land that they had left behind, they would have had opportunity to return. But as it is, they desire a better country, that is, a heavenly one. Therefore God is not ashamed to be called their God; indeed, he has prepared a city for them. (Heb. 11:8–16)

Finally, we come to the Letter of James, often presented in the New Testament as complement or even antithesis to Paul's theology of grace. This letter issues a call to put faith into action with the claim that faith without works is dead. (This caused Martin Luther to refer to this book as an epistle of straw and to wish for its excision from the canon.) In this text, because faith is seen as empty, as dead without works, it may seem to contradict what Paul says in

Epistle: Just another word for a letter.

Romans. The author of the Letter of James cites Genesis 22, the story of the sacrifice of Isaac, a story not mentioned by Paul in Romans. That perplexing, even troubling story is offered as an illustration of the experience of obedience and absolute dependence on God. It illustrates in some ways what Paul is saying about the need for trust, and the promise of resurrection emerging from what might seem like a dead end.

So faith by itself, if it has no works, is dead. But someone will say, "You have faith and I have works." Show me your faith apart from your works, and I by my works will show you my faith. You believe that God is one; you do well. Even the demons believe—and shudder. Do you want to be shown, you senseless person, that faith apart from works is barren? Was not our ancestor Abraham justified by works when he offered his son Isaac on the altar? You see that faith was active along with his works, and faith was brought to completion by the works. Thus the scripture was fulfilled that says, "Abraham believed God, and it was reckoned to him as righteousness," and he was called the friend of God. You see that a person is justified by works and not by faith alone. (James 2:17–24)

The Theme of Blessing for All

When Paul chooses to focus on the story of Abraham, he is offering a vision of God's saving action offered in surprising ways, reaching beyond boundaries. The example offered by Abraham, someone who uniquely represents both Jew and Gentile, speaks of blessing from God, or the grace of God that comes through the promise. In the book of Genesis, we hear the promise that comes to Abraham. "In you, all the families of the earth will be blessed." That promise, offered without condition or limit, is what Paul believes is revealed in Jesus Christ, indeed fulfilled in him. It finds expression in the community that represents his body, opening the door for ever broader inclusion. The hope brought with that revelation will be addressed in the next chapter, as Paul's argument continues to build.

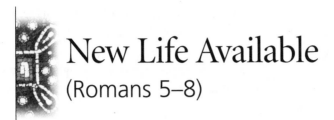

## CHAPTER FIVE

New Life Available
(Romans 5–8)

When Adam ate the irrevocable apple,
Thou saw'st beyond death the resurrection
of the dead.

—C.S. LEWIS, *POEMS*[31]

It is in this way that the doctrine of origi-
nal sin is the culmination of the revealed
understanding of being human: the shape
of divine forgiveness revealed in the resur-
rection of Jesus shows itself to stretch into
our congenial involvement with death.
The doctrine of original sin is the doctrine
of the un-necessity of death.

—JAMES ALISON, *THE JOY OF BEING WRONG*[32]

What Does It Mean to Be Justified?
(Romans 5:1–11)

When we speak about someone who is justified, what does
that language conjure up for the reader? Perhaps it suggests
someone who is within his or her rights to do something.
Perhaps it seems closely related to the idea of being righteous, another key word in Paul's letter, which is often
understood to be a matter of being right, a matter of
exhibiting right behavior. That easily spills over into being
self-righteous, a divisive attribute, a less than attractive

quality in religious people, perhaps the attribute of Puritans, who have been defined as those people who are unhappy because somebody somewhere is having a good time.

When Paul speaks about being justified or being righteous, as he does throughout this letter, he is not focused on human activity, achievement, intention, or will. He describes righteousness as something God does, a gracious and powerful transformation available to all people, indeed needed by all people. Paul speaks about the hope of restored relationship between God and humanity, relationship broken by the hubris expressed in idolatry, leading people to see themselves as the center of the universe and in the process getting in the way of community.

We continue our conversation with this letter by moving into a new section, a critical hinge in Paul's argument. He sums up the transformational power of God's justifying activity in Romans 5, beginning with the word "therefore." It's been said that whenever we see the word "therefore" in one of Paul's letters, especially in the Letter to the Romans, we need to ask what the "therefore" is there for. (It will come up in several places. Take note of when it appears. It indicates an important transition or conclusion.) Paul builds on the argument that right relationship with God is available to all, saying that we are justified by faith. Perhaps he has in mind the kind of faith exhibited by Abraham who prior to any explicit awareness or articulation of the law, trusted in God's ability to fulfill the divine promise. It is possible that Paul is talking about the faith exhibited by Jesus in his death and resurrection, which only makes the divine initiative more significant. Perhaps he has both dynamics in mind, pointing to the synergy of God's gracious activity and human faithful embrace.

So what is the significance of the "therefore" at this juncture? The act of justification affected by God in Christ, a gracious divine initiative offered apart from human merit, effort, intention, or will, brings peace with God, providing access to the "grace in which we stand." The theme of peace with God underscores the understanding that justification and righteousness are primarily about healing of relationship that has been broken, bringing together God and humanity when that relationship had been marked by separation. As noted later in the Letter to the Romans and in other letters attributed to

Paul, the effect of that reconciliation brings transformed relationship between God and humanity.

It also leads to healthy relationships in the community, in the church, and in the world. The theme of peace and reconciliation is woven throughout Paul's letters, notably in the Corinthian correspondence in which Paul sounds themes familiar to readers of Romans. In a passage often read in the Ash Wednesday liturgy, Paul writes:

> If anyone is in Christ, there is a new creation: everything old has passed away; see everything has become new! All this is from God, who reconciled us to himself through Christ, and has given us the ministry of reconciliation, that is, in Christ, God was reconciling the world to himself, not counting their trespasses against them and entrusting the message of reconciliation to us. So we are ambassadors for Christ, since God is making his appeal through us; we entreat you on behalf of Christ, be reconciled to God. For our sake he made him to be sin who knew no sin, so that in him we might become the righteousness of God. (2 Cor. 5:17–21)

All of this leads Paul to say that we boast in our hope of sharing the glory of God, a reiteration of the thesis of the letter in which Paul says he is not ashamed of the gospel. Boasting is permissible in this context, boasting in the hope of sharing the glory of God, the glory that those who have fallen short are kept from receiving. This hope of sharing God's glory will find fullest expression in chapter 8, one of the most hopeful passages in the New Testament. Paul will take it even a step further by saying that because of this transforming gospel of grace, there is grace available to navigate the sufferings of the present time, to make sense of how God is at work, even claiming a redemptive dimension to suffering. Grace has the power to make that happen.

For Paul, suffering produces character, which produces hope, which does not disappoint because God's love has been given in our hearts. In this way, Paul makes sense of what God is doing in the world, and why the Christian community is experiencing challenge. He moves from faith (v. 1) to hope (vv. 2–5) to love, echoing the concluding words of 1 Corinthians 13 where Paul speaks about the abiding power of faith, hope, and love, ending with the affirmation that the greatest of these is love. That love is seen in this passage as God's active demonstration of love for us in that "while we were still sinners Christ died for us." That's the basis for boasting in God "through our Lord Jesus Christ, through whom we have received reconciliation." That love is seen in the grace of Christ's death, understood by Paul as an act of justification with salvific effect, marking deliverance from the wrath of God, bringing about reconciliation. With that affirmation, Paul continues to explore why reconciliation is needed, again entering into conversation with his own Scriptures, going back to the first chapters of Genesis.

What's Adam Got to Do with It?
(Romans 5:12–21)

As Paul writes in conversation with this community, he anticipates their questions, expressed repeatedly in various ways. They are questions pertaining to the following mystery: If the gospel is really a matter of God's initiative, God's power, why didn't this all work out better? Where did sin come from? Why was there a break in relationship at all? Note the ways in which this letter, which explores the faithfulness of God, and even on occasion seems to put God to the test, poses questions that we still are asking, as we wonder why bad things happen to good people, as we wonder with the Bible in one hand and the newspaper in another about the goodness and sovereignty of God.

Paul provides an answer by comparing and contrasting Adam and Christ, each representative of humanity. Paul refers to Adam in other letters (1 Cor. 15, in particular). It is not entirely clear how Paul understands the role of Adam in what has come to be known as the doctrine of original sin, set forth by Augustine and developed by others throughout the history of the church, often finding its warrant in passages like this one. But Paul makes the claim that in the story of Adam, especially as described in Genesis 3, the dominion of sin, the power of sin, was introduced into creation, allowing the power of death to enter creation (Gen. 3:19, 22–24). It's all about power.

The important point for Paul is that Christ's offering, Christ's activity, has superseded the effect of Adam's action. In Adam, the power of sin apparently broke into the world. Alienation between God and humanity emerged (5:12–14). The free gift that has been revealed in Christ has greater power than the effect of Adam's transgression. Paul does not specifically name that transgression, but mindful of Paul's thematic interests, one could imagine it has to do with the persistent, pernicious tendency to boast, as seen in the Garden of Eden when the man and the woman decide to eat the fruit, egged on by the serpent who tells them that they will become like gods. As C. K. Barrett notes,[33] the serpent had cast doubt upon God's truthfulness and goodness, so that Adam sets himself in the place of God.

Paul does not say exactly how sin has been handed down, whether it became part of human DNA. Paul does not teach direct genetic or biological identity between Adam and descendants, which seems to be implied in the nearly contemporaneous 4 Ezra (7:11-14). We have no sense that Paul is even concerned about what we would consider the literal historicity of the Genesis story. That's not a question he would ask and there's a lot we don't know about how Paul understood the roles of Adam and Christ.

But he clearly sees a contrast between the two, unfolded in a series of comparisons. Many died because of Adam. Many will live because of Christ. The judgment of God leads to a decree of condemnation. The gift of God brings a decree of righteousness. One man's sin caused death to rule. Those who have been justified, those who have been made righteous now rule. One man's trespass led to judgment for all. One man's offering leads to acquittal that is life for all. One man's disobedience causes all human beings to be established as sinners. Jesus's obedience leads to the possibility of being righteous, being set in right relationship. A new power has been unleashed in the death and resurrection of Jesus Christ. Paul announces a new day, a new reality.

Life in Christ (Romans 6:1–23)

So how is it that we live into this new life, this new reality? Another way to say this: How do we live into the grace we have received? What does grace look like when it goes to work in the world, in our lives? It's the question asked in any church where sacramental life is upheld, where we claim that God acts by grace.

Take, for example, the sacrament that Paul will describe in this sixth chapter, the sacrament of baptism, a sacrament of new birth. It is a gift, but if a child or an adult is brought to the font for that holy rite, and never goes out into the world to live out the Baptismal Covenant, or does go out into the world but ignores the promises made in the service, then one might inquire into the meaning of that grace. Take, for example, the sacrament of holy communion, the grace of bread and wine transformed into Christ's presence, but really only meaningful once taken into the world, launched by the dismissal that is arguably the most important part of every service of Holy Eucharist, equipping saints for ministry. (One church posted the following message over the exit of the nave: The worship is over. The service begins.) Take, for example, the sacrament of marriage, proclaimed as a grace, a sacrament, a gift of union when blessed. Such a gift only has meaning if that new relationship goes to work in the world, expressed in the union between those two being married, expressed in fulfillment of the commitment to honor one another.

Once again, as in earlier passages, Paul anticipates questions from this congregation, questions still being asked in conversation with Scripture. If all is dependent on God's gracious activity, God's initiative, God's intervention, how then are we meant to live? Shouldn't we sin a lot more so that grace will abound? The last chapters (chapters 12–16) of Paul's Letter to the Romans explore these questions in depth, with specific and practical application. But Paul gets a jump on the discussion here in chapter 6 by talking about baptism. Paul explains baptism in ways that have been repeated throughout the history of the church. This rite not only reenacts the narrative of Holy Week, Jesus's death and resurrection. It is also a rite that provides an understanding of how followers of Christ are to live out their lives in the world as resurrection people, in response to grace that has transformed them.

One might ask then: Does the sacrament itself then become a work, a human doing? Paul has tapped into a question that probably accompanies all religious observance. How do we avoid seeing our religious practice as something that makes us different than others, more worthy, more holy, more deserving of grace? The ego will never give it a rest. We always try to figure out how we are better than others. That's why we are so utterly dependent on grace. In baptism, we are called to die to that way of thinking. It is a spiritual practice, taking practice in the sense that we need to be intentional about it. It is a way of life that paradoxically involves a dying with Christ, a dying to the ego, an idea that Paul presents in the Letter to the Galatians where he speaks of being crucified with Christ:

> For through the law I died to the law, so that I might live to God. I have been crucified with Christ, and it is no longer I who live, but it is Christ who lives in me. And the life I now live in the flesh I live by faith in the Son of God, who loved me and gave himself for me. (Gal. 2:19–20)

Thanks be to God, the drama enacted in the liturgy of baptism is not only a matter of dying with Christ, a dying to ego, a dying to the boasting that tries to set us in the place of God, and above other people. It also intends the promise of resurrection, integral to Paul's theology expressed powerfully in two related passages from the epistles attributed to Paul.

> But God, who is rich in mercy, out of the great love with which he loved us even when we were dead through our trespasses, made us alive together with Christ—by grace you have been saved—and raised us up with him and seated us with him in the heavenly places in Christ Jesus. (Eph. 2:4–6)

> You were buried with him in baptism, you were also raised with him through faith in the power of God, who raised him from the dead. And when you were dead in trespasses and the uncircumcision of your flesh, God made you alive together with him, when he forgave us all our trespasses. (Col. 2:12–13)

Paul in the sixth chapter of Romans invites the congregation to experience this resurrected life, a new way of being, a new lifestyle freed from the power of sin, the power of ego, and the toxicity of boasting. In baptism, in our identification with Christ, we are freed from the dominion of sin, no longer under the law that reveals our powerlessness,

Paul in the sixth chapter of Romans invites the congregation to experience this resurrected life, a new way of being, a new lifestyle freed from the power of sin, the power of ego, and the toxicity of boasting.

our inability to live in reconciled relationship. Instead we are set on a pathway toward a new life empowered by grace.

Paul has to repeat the question in v. 15. Should we sin because we are not under the law but under grace? This brings to mind Bob Dylan who, at a stage in his life when he embraced an evangelical expression of Christianity, wrote songs that reflected that religious experience. One of those songs repeated the refrain: "You gotta serve somebody."[34] The point of the song was simple. Every one of us serves somebody or something. The idea of independence is overrated. We are not free agents. We all worship something. We all serve somebody.

Paul makes a similar point, presenting the truth that we all live in some kind of servitude, an echo of the opening lines of the epistle where he describes himself as a slave or servant of Christ. He points to the paradox by which we discover freedom in service. He admits, as he does in several places, that there are limits to his analogy, but it is useful enough to share and to say to his audience that while they were formerly slaves of sin, they now have become slaves of righteousness.

That service, indeed that slavery, is part of a process of moving to a deeper holiness, growing spiritually, not as a way of earning God's affection, not as a way of setting oneself above others, mindful of how the ego has a heyday with religious people. By going all the way back to Adam, he says that slavery to sin results in death, in separation from God, in broken relationship with God, while the life that is described as being enslaved to God will unfold to new, eternal life. Note the contrast in Romans 6:23: "The wages of sin is death, but the free gift of God is eternal life in Christ Jesus our Lord." To underscore this dynamic, Paul talks about the power of the law. As we move into the seventh chapter, he shares in a distinctively personal way how that power has affected his own life.

The Limits of the Law (Romans 7:1–13)

In this seventh chapter, Paul addresses those in his audience who know the law, making specific reference to marriage law. This analogy to marriage law (described by some commentators as tangled[35]) provides the basis of an analogy to the transformative event that has taken place with the death and resurrection of Jesus. Paul argues that once a spouse has died, the surviving spouse is no longer bound by the laws that previously guided the life of the couple. Paul envisions a new day, a new life discharged from the old law.

Building on the notion of baptism presented in chapter 6, with the imagery of dying to an old way of life, Paul says that resurrection brings a new reality. That new life which emerges in baptism has rendered them dead to the demands and the judgment, even the curse, of the law (Gal. 2:19, 3:13). Those who claim the grace that has come in Christ find themselves free from the claims of the law. They now serve the life of the Spirit. (See 2 Cor. 3:7–18 for another discussion of the law and the Spirit, with particular reference to Moses.)

It is Paul's way of arguing that the law is not bad, not a mistake or a failure. Rather, in Christ, God is doing a new thing that changes the dynamics. Now that we are "discharged from the law" (v. 6), we are dead to that which held us captive, slaves not under the old written code but slaves to the new life of the spirit. This whole chapter will be a reminder of a key element stated in that thesis back in Romans 1:16–17: the gospel is about liberating power that counters the inimical powers which hold human beings captive. The power of the law aroused sinful passions, most notably the tendency toward claiming we are like gods.

Paul repeatedly brings up the subject of the relationship between the law and sin, He takes care to separate the two. He is mindful of the state of humanity held under the sway of sin, and the inability of the law to free humanity from that influence. It is not to say that the law is bad, or that it is at fault (v. 7). Rather, the law provided an opportunity for the power of sin to take hold, just as religious observance holds out the temptation that one group will consider themselves better than another, falling prey to the power of ego. But for a number of reasons, Paul wants to assert that the law is not at fault. According to Paul, it is described as "holy and just and good," though the power of sin worked through the law to create an opportunity for sin's power to go to work. The law was insufficient to overcome the power of that sin taking hold.

Paul's Experience with the Law
(Romans 7:14–25)

The discussion of law, the back and forth about the relationship between law and sin, can seem tangled. With that in mind, in the last half of the chapter, Paul gets personal. He describes his own ongoing struggles in a passage of distinctive transparency. He talks about the gap between the good life to which he has been called by the law, and his own powerlessness to live into that good and holy and just thing. In verse 14, Paul uses the pronoun "I" to share his own struggle, his understanding that the law is indeed a spiritual reality. He admits that he is of the flesh, noting the flesh as that sphere of influence where sin has dominion. (Be warned: the dichotomy between flesh and spirit has created a dualistic approach throughout the history of the church, a dichotomy that has not always been helpful in theological discussion.)

Read out loud, the passage is almost comical. Paul is in a bit of a loop:

> I do not do the good I want, but the evil I do not want is what I do. Now if I do what I do not want, it is no longer I that do it, but sin that dwells within me. (Rom. 7:19–20)

If people chuckle in church when this comes up in the lectionary, it may be because the language has a circular quality. It may also be because we see ourselves in this mirror of Scripture. We know this to be true of our experience, that what we do and what we want to do are not always the same. Anyone who has dealt with compulsion, temptation, or addiction can attest to the gap between intention and action. Anyone who has ever battled to control what we say or to dispel resentment that persists can attest to this dynamic. We are often powerless over our actions. Paul describes an evil power, always close at hand, a force creating captivity to the power of sin making him act in ways that he knows are destructive.

Paul ends by claiming need for rescue, describing himself as a wretched man, cognizant that the best he had to offer, the resources available to him, the system of religious principle, was not powerful enough to close the gap between what he was doing and being and what he was called to do and be. He knew what it meant to fall short. Apparently at the end of his rope, Paul appeals for help and sees that help coming from beyond himself, from a higher power, God working through Jesus Christ.

Paul sees himself as the battleground for dueling powers, spirit against flesh, a slave to the law of God, a slave to the law of the spirit. It is a depiction of the ongoing struggle all people face. Luther spoke about this dynamic when he noted that we are saints and sinners at the same time. One bishop described it this way: I never met a motive that wasn't mixed.

The fact is that the Christian life, with its eschatological focus, is complicated, captured in the phrase which says that we live in the not yet/already. We are works in progress. The discrepancy between what we are and what we are called to be, as individuals and a church, calls us to ever deeper transformation. That transformation will be unfolded in the eighth chapter, which deals directly with the suffering of the present age, and concludes with a soaring vision of the power of God's love to liberate, so much so that the eighth chapter has been called the pinnacle of the New Testament.

Life in the Spirit (Romans 8:1–39)

Once again, we come to a key moment in the flow of this letter, signaled by the return of that word "therefore." In stark contrast to the wrenching declaration of his own wretchedness at the end of chapter 7, Paul announces that there is no condemnation in Christ Jesus. Pause here and note how different that is from most people's experience of religious institutions. How would our regard for God, for neighbor, for ourselves be transformed if we really embraced the notion that there is no condemnation?

Paul affirms that in Christ, God has done what the law was not able to do, "the just requirement of the law fulfilled according to the Spirit." A resurrected life flows from the power of the resurrection of Jesus, so that those with ears to hear are called to set their minds on the things of the spirit. Compare Colossians 3:1–3, a text often read in Easter liturgy: "If you have been raised with Christ, seek the things that are above, where Christ is, seated at the right hand of God. Set your minds on things that are above, not on things that are on the earth, for you have died and your life is hidden with Christ in God." It's all about discovering a new mindfulness, apparently.

Paul finds another way to talk about this study in contrasts, comparing life in the flesh to life in the spirit. In talking about the person whose mind is set on the flesh, it is not simply the case that such a person is hostile to God, but that such a person is unable to enter into right relationship with God. There is a need for transforming power, a power greater than human power. Paul found that power in his own life in the resurrected Christ. In verse 9, Paul addresses his audience directly, telling them that such power is available to them, that the one who raised Christ from the dead will raise them as well.

Paul makes a shift, arguing his point in another way, part of this theological symphony, one piece in the mosaic of his argument. Earlier he had noted that everyone is a slave, either a slave of sin or a slave of righteousness. (Remember Bob Dylan: "You gotta serve somebody."[36]) Now he compares and contrasts a spirit of slavery with a spirit of adoption, claiming that life in the spirit will usher in new relationship, no longer characterized by servitude, but by familial relationship. That relationship is marked by love, a spirit of adoption that allows for the intimate appeal to the Father, an Aramaic term that Jesus may have used in appeal to the one he called Father (Mark 14:36). It is also a term used in the Letter to the Galatians where the theme of adoption is repeated (Gal. 4:6). Paul expresses an intimacy of relationship, a closer connection. In the journey of the Christian life, discipleship is so closely linked with Christ that suffering along with Christ will lead to the glorification that Christ experienced.

With that, the topic shifts to the reality of suffering in the lives of the faithful, a timeless question woven throughout this letter, an experience familiar to Paul and to this congregation in Rome. Paul contrasts the suffering of this time and the glory that is to be revealed. It is no wonder that this passage is often selected for the Burial Office in the Book of Common Prayer, where it is used to bring a spirit of hope to people suffering greatest loss. Paul addresses the congregation of the faithful set in the wider context of creation. Creation wrestles with its own sense of bondage, awaiting freedom, groaning in the present as it anticipates giving birth to something new. (Contemporary readers will hear this passage in new ways based on the ecological challenges facing our planet, unprecedented threatening dynamics that would have been inconceivable in the first century.) Paul's language is similar to apocalyptic writings found in the gospels: for instance, in Matthew 24:8 or Mark 13:8, where end-times are compared to birth pangs, or in John 16:21, where Jesus speaks to his disciples in a farewell address, noting that they will experience pain now but the advent of new life will usher in a time of joy.

In the midst of the recognition of the brokenness of the world, Paul reflects on the power of hope, the spirit leading into a vision of a greater possibility, the anticipation of adoption, of new, healed, and safe relationship. In that in-between time in which we all live, before that hope is realized, Paul claims the power of the Spirit present with us, acting as the comforter, the advocate, the *paraclete* (one who comes alongside) that Jesus promised to the disciples at the Last Supper (see John 14–15). When the Spirit intercedes with sighs too deep for words, Paul notes that there is much we cannot understand, much we cannot verbalize, much that cannot be contained in human constructs, much that will call us to rely fully on the mystery of the grace of God, much that will call us to that absolute dependence, indeed to faith.

Perhaps the greatest mystery is this: Paul claims God's presence and providence in all that transpires. All things work together for good. While that truth is not always easy to affirm, for any number of reasons, Paul argues that nothing exists outside the providence of God's grace and love. This section provides a clear affirmation of God's sovereignty, which presents a challenging theological conversation as we consider the relationship between God's power and human choice or free will. Calvin based a theology of predestination on this idea that some were predestined for salvation and others were not. In the next section, chapters 9–11, several passages will seem to make this argument. Our conversation with Scripture calls us to wrestle with this point of view.

Whatever sense we make of that mysterious notion of predestination, in this context Paul uses it to develop a progression, a spiritual continuum. He speaks of those who are called, those who God foreknew, who were predestined to be conformed to the image of his

Son, the firstborn within a large family. Paul aims to emphasize God's activity, not a response of human religion, but the mysterious and gracious initiative of a God whose ways our higher than our ways, a vision of God's action that holds a hope that all will ultimately be called. As has been said: "Everything will be okay in the end. If it's not okay, it's not the end." In the closing verses of this chapter, with an expression of hope, Paul affirms what he said in chapter 5 that in spite of the evidence, in spite of current events, the love of God will win.

The love of God is greater than any power. It will ultimately hold sway. In the end, there is nothing that can separate us from the love of God.

There is plenty to argue about in this chapter, plenty that is confusing, plenty to generate lively conversation. The arguments that Paul makes have moved in many directions and can be challenged on many counts. But we miss the radical vision, the transformative power of this letter if we fail to note Paul's central thesis. The love of God is greater than any power. It will ultimately hold sway. In the end, there is nothing that can separate us from the love of God.

Conclude your reading of this chapter with some quiet time in reflection on these closing verses, which may explain why some have called Romans 8 the pinnacle of the New Testament:

> What then are we to say about these things? If God is for us, who is against us? He who did not withhold his own Son, but gave him up for all of us, will he not with him also give us everything else? Who will bring any charge against God's elect? It is God who justifies. Who is to condemn? It is Christ Jesus, who died, yes, who was raised, who is at the right hand of God, who indeed intercedes for us. Who will separate us from the love of Christ? Will hardship, or distress, or persecution, or famine, or nakedness, or peril, or sword? As it is written, "For your sake we are being killed all day long; we are accounted as sheep to be slaughtered." No, in all these things we are more than conquerors through him who loved us. For I am convinced that neither death, nor life, nor angels, nor rulers, nor things present, nor things to come, nor powers, nor height, nor depth, nor anything else in all creation, will be able to separate us from the love of God in Christ Jesus our Lord. (Rom. 8:31–39)

## CHAPTER SIX

God on Trial: The Mystery of the Plan for Salvation for All
(Romans 9–11)

*There's a wideness to God's mercy, like the
wideness of the sea.
There is kindness in his justice which is
more than liberty.*[37]

This next section of the letter puts us in conversation with
a few of the most challenging chapters in the New Testament. Some have viewed them as digression, a detour.
There's a temptation to hit the fast-forward button, moving
from the soaring affirmation of the love of God at the end
of chapter 8, diving right into the call to respond in the
beginning of chapter 12. But chapters 9–11 provide an
important bridge, addressing questions that Paul has been
circling in a variety of ways from the beginning of his letter.

Paul has been exploring the mystery of grace, the pri-
macy of God's initiative balanced against the fact that
God's will, God's loving intention seems to have been in
some way thwarted. Paul has spoken about the ways that
human beings have fallen short of the glory of God, a universal dynamic that separates all from relationship with
God. We can see what that says about human beings, the
results painfully evident in the daily news.

It's more difficult to understand what that says about
God. So the questions fly: Did the promises made to Israel

in previous generations mean anything? Is God faithful? Does the Jewish community have any advantage? If they were unfaithful, does that nullify the faithfulness of God? Has God given up on Israel? Did God have a change of mind, of heart? If human injustice illuminates the justice of God, how can God inflict wrath because of that? Is God the God of the Jewish people only, or is God the God of all people? Think about how these questions might get translated into our own day. We'll offer questions at the end of this book to help reflect on that. Paul tackles these kinds of questions in these three chapters in Romans (chapters 9–11).

While there's a strong tradition in American Christianity that focuses on individual religious experience (e.g., Jesus as personal savior), Paul addresses two distinct constituencies present in this Roman congregation, represented in many of the first-century congregations that Paul sought to pastor. He explores the relationship of Jewish and Gentile communities to God, which is another way of talking about the call to righteousness, as we note again that righteousness is more about relationship than rules.

To review, the first three chapters of the book have focused on the righteousness of God in terms of impartiality. All of humanity stands in the same relationship to God, all having fallen short. In subsequent chapters, Paul characterizes God's response in terms of justification, or as some have referred to this divine activity, as rightwising, which allows us to speak of the righteousness of God in a proactive way.

In these three chapters (Rom. 9–11) the righteousness of God is exhibited in the ways that God shows mercy to all. Seen in this light, chapters 9–11 serve not as detour or diversion but as a climax to the previous eight chapters, an attempt to resolve or reconcile any number of tensions. In these chapters, Paul will seek to reconcile the promises made to Israel (4:16–17) with Israel's apparent rejection of those promises (10:21). He will seek to reconcile the priority of Israel, a sign of God's election (9:4–5) with the focus on Gentile mission, a sign of the universality of the gospel which holds the promise of justification and life for all (5:18). He will note the centrality of faith as God's work (9:6), standing in contrast to human effort, responsibility, and accomplishment (2:6). Paul will try to weave answers to these questions to present a coherent vision of the gospel he is called to proclaim. He has his work cut out for him. It will not be an easy task.

Looking at it another way, chapter 8 ended with the unequivocal declaration that all things work together for good, that "if God is for us, who can be against us?" So where does Israel stand, as a covenant community, in the unfolding of these promises? If God's electing purpose cannot be thwarted, why has Israel apparently rejected that purpose, refusing to embrace the gospel to which Paul has committed his life? The stakes are high. The meaning of promise, covenant, and election are in question.

Paul struggles with two competing dynamics. First, he observes contemporary Jewish rejection of the good news about Jesus as Messiah and Lord. How could his people reject a message that had become so significant to him? Second, he notes that there is Gentile acceptance of that message. So he has to ask questions like: Who really are God's people? It's a reiteration of questions expressed in chapter 3 about the true Israel. Paul asks: Has God been faithful in the promises God has made? As will become apparent in these three chapters, this is not a hypothetical concern for Paul, but a source of personal sorrow. Even though he has claimed that nothing can separate from the love of God, he himself would be willing to be cut off from the love of God for the sake of his people.

In these passages, Paul enters into conversation with the Scriptures of his tradition, trying to make sense out of the experience he sees around him. Just to offer a "heads-up," by the time we arrive at the end of this section we may well conclude that Paul doesn't come up with a satisfactory or a logical answer. But the fact that he struggles with these questions is significant.

In our contemporary context, we struggle with them as well. That leads to a note of caution as we launch into this passage. Paul wrote this letter in the middle of the first century. Gentiles were just being welcomed into the church. The Roman Empire had not yet embraced the Christian faith. Both Jews and Christians experienced persecution, albeit for different reasons. We come to this letter long after Constantine shifted the political dynamic. Christianity then became the religion of the empire, and Judaism a marginalized religion. We read this letter after two thousand years of Western Christianity marked by persistent anti-Semitism. We read this letter on the other side of the Holocaust, an event perpetrated by ostensibly Christian nations on the Jewish people. We read these passages about Jewish/Gentile relationships through a lens that Paul could not have been able to even imagine. We read this passage through the lens of contemporary globalization that calls us to consider God's activity in different faith traditions.

As we have said, our conversation with Scripture must explore what these passages said to the people who first read them. We must also explore what they say to us in a different historical context. We must engage not only Scripture, but tradition, reason, and experience to note the difference.

The Problem of Israel's Unbelief
(Romans 9:1–5)

In these verses, Paul affirms his own affinity and connection with Israel, as the recipient of God's blessing, to which Paul alluded in the passages about Abraham. Paul speaks in a deeply personal way, framed with sorrow and anguish, even offering to sacrifice himself for the sake of his own people, his kindred according to the flesh. With echoes of the Hebrew Scripture (Exod. 4:22–23, which speaks of Israel as God's firstborn, and Hosea 11:1 in which God says: "When Israel was a child, I loved him, and out of Egypt I called my son."), Paul identifies a special place for Israel in his vision of salvation history. He refers to their adoption, the glory, the covenants, the giving of the law, the worship, the promises, the patriarchs, and ultimately the context out of which the Messiah comes, the one now ascended and triumphant and blessed forever, all of that sealed with a resounding Amen. If there was any sense that Paul was abandoning the relationship that Israel had with the God of the Hebrew Scriptures, Paul makes it clear in this opening blessing that Israel occupies a special place, which will prompt conversation for us about what it might mean in our world to be considered chosen people.

Has God's Promise to Israel Failed?
(Romans 9:6–29)

In this section, Paul faces that question head on, beginning with the statement that the word of God has not failed. (Again, the faithfulness of God seems to be at stake.) As Paul enters into conversation with his own Scriptures, and at the same time, anticipates the questions of this congregation, he poses questions that may come to us in our own conversation with Scripture. He explores the mystery of why faith takes root in some people, and why it does not take hold in others, questions that can and should be asked in contemporary faith communities.

In order to make sense of the tensions he senses, Paul will redefine what it means to be Israel, which raises challenging questions about who gets to define the community. Paul rises to the defense of God in the following way. Identification with Israel is not a matter of physical descent. True descendants of Abraham are those who embrace the promise. Paul draws on stories from Genesis, notably stories preceding the giving of the law, unfolding in the promise that Abraham and Sarah would have a son, noting that while Abraham had more than one son, the promise was carried on through Isaac. As Isaac and Rebekah had twins, Jacob and Esau, the promise was carried through the younger twin, Jacob, whose name means supplanter, and who apparently did very little to distinguish himself as more righteous than his brother.

The determinative principle in the narrative of Jacob and Esau is that God's purpose of election unfolds not by works, but by God's call, God's freedom to make that call, through promise. Like it or not, understand it or not, Paul's argument has led him to full reliance on God who chooses to show mercy according to divine purpose and call, based not on human will or merit. Paul seeks to "establish that Scripture has always told stories that illustrate the selective character of God's grace."[38]

This point becomes the occasion in the letter when Paul makes explicit reference to the Exodus, the central story of the Hebrew Scripture. He compares Moses and Pharoah, noting that God, in God's freedom, hardens Pharaoh's heart for the purpose of the saving liberation of his people and for the proclamation of God's message throughout the whole world. Our conversation with Scripture might cause us to ask whether Pharoah had a choice in the matter, whether it was predetermined how he would act, whether he could be held accountable. Was Pharoah handed over to his obduracy? As we're mulling that over, Paul picks up the metaphor of potter and clay, a metaphor echoing passages in Isaiah (29:16; 45:9), Jeremiah (18:6), and the book of Wisdom (15:7). The metaphor claims that it is within God's right to make vessels according to divine purpose, some for destruction and some for showing mercy.

This whole chapter has been an attempt by Paul to explore the mystery of those who exhibit faith and those who don't. This is hardly a new question. Paul has traced the dynamic back to the first stories in Genesis. God's free purpose, God's election has been demonstrated in God's mysterious freedom to act, evident in the story of Isaac chosen over Ishmael, Jacob chosen over Esau, in the hardening of Pharoah's heart. God's election opened the doors for the formation of Israel. His ongoing determination of a special role for Israel is expressed in the vision of a faithful remnant, a vision presented in the prophecies of Hosea and Isaiah.

The Nature of True Righteousness (Romans 9:30–33, 10:1–21)

So what went wrong? According to Paul, Gentiles who did nothing to earn the justifying action of God were declared righteous, obtaining the righteousness of faith. Israel, who strove for the righteousness based on the law, did not embrace it, but rather stumbled over it, faithlessly placing confidence in their own works. Again, while Paul does not seem entirely able to explain this dynamic, he asserts that it has precedent in the Hebrew Scriptures. As he enters into conversation with this Roman congregation, he seeks to illustrate that the freedom of God upholds the faithfulness of God.

Paul claims that Gentiles have become part of the righteous people based on faith (9:30). How does Paul explain that so many of his Jewish brothers and sisters have failed to embrace this message? In his own conversation with Scripture, Paul invites Scripture to debate with itself. He compares Leviticus 18:5, which says that the person who does these things (i.e., lives by the law) will live by them, with Deuteronomy 30:11–14, which articulates a righteousness by faith, whereby the "word is very near," on the lips and in the heart, citing passages from the Hebrew Scriptures which uphold the righteousness of faith. The Good News, the gospel that Paul proclaims and that is deeply rooted in the Jewish community, is now accessible to all.

The rejection of the promised one was predicted, for example, in passages from Isaiah, chapters 49–60, a section of that prophetic book that has appeared in many places in Paul's letter. In quoting the first verse of Isaiah 53 (as he does in verse 16) Paul suggests that this should not come as a surprise. The prophet Isaiah predicted long ago that not all would obey or embrace the good news. The psalmist spoke of how the news went out into all the world. Moses predicted that outsiders would make insiders jealous of a relationship with God, and again Isaiah explains that God has been found by those who did not seek, by those who did not ask, unmerited favor, grace. The section closes as the God of Israel says of the people: "All day long I have held out my hands to a disobedient and contrary people."

So does that mean that Israel has lost its chance, has lost its future? Is this an argument for the long-held Christian belief in supersessionism, i.e., that Christianity supersedes, and perhaps invalidates, the covenantal relationship between God and Israel? This is a question that contemporary interfaith dialogue has had to address.

Israel's Rejection Is Not Final
(Romans 11:1–16)

Paul's personal experience is drawn in again. He notes that he is an Israelite, a descendant of Abraham, a member of the tribe of Benjamin. God has preserved a remnant, evoking God's answer to Elijah found in 1 Kings 19, where Elijah, indulging in self-pity, imagines he is the only one who has found the right path. Maybe Paul felt that way at times. The divine response to Elijah is a call to trust, to imagine a broader vision than his self-absorption could afford, discovering the remnant has been preserved, a group marked by faithfulness, established by grace. The answer for Paul is that an elect group, a

chosen group, has obtained this righteousness, this right relationship. Yet, at the same time, there was an obdurate group that refused
to see. Paul offers two texts from the Hebrew Scriptures to denote
this mysterious dynamic. First, from Isaiah (6:9–10) Paul cites a passage describing those who have eyes that would not see and ears that
would not hear. The psalmist (Ps. 69) indicates that their eyes were
purposefully darkened.

It is interesting to note how many times these passages from Isaiah
6 and Psalm 69 surface in the New Testament. They appear in the
gospels, in the Acts of the Apostles, and in many of Paul's letters as
ways to note (but not necessarily explain) the human response of
unbelief, pointing to the purposeful hiddenness of God. We may not
be satisfied that these passages explain the mystery of acceptance and
rejection of faith. But Paul in his argument, in his conversation with
Scripture, sees these passages as a way to hold together the freedom
of God and the free will of human beings.

Paul speaks to the Gentiles in this passage, as an apostle, one sent
to them to explain his mission to them. Again, going back to Paul's
concern for the unity of the church, he may be addressing Gentiles
in the Roman congregation who disparage their Jewish brothers
and sisters. He envisions that these two groups can be forged into
one community of faith, based on a common experience of the
righteousness of God.

As he turns his attention to Gentiles, his mission is not about the
rejection of Israel that might be construed from other texts. It is not
the angry turning from Israel depicted, for instance, in Acts 18:6
("When they [the Jews] opposed and reviled him, in protest he
[Paul] shook the dust from his clothes and said to them, "Your blood
be on your own heads! I am innocent. From now on I will go to the
Gentiles."). It is not the denunciation of "Judaizers" in the Letter to
the Galatians, where he addressed a community that sought to rein-
state observance of certain ritual laws. (In that letter, for Paul, the law
takes on an almost demonic quality.)

Paul wants to avert any sense that Gentiles might presume that
their own spiritual insight makes them superior to their Jewish
brothers and sisters. So he suggests that there is a divine plan for

these two communities, by which the power of the resurrection might still come to those who seem to have rejected the faith Paul proclaims (as seen in verses 12 and 15). Paul says that if their rejection brings about the inclusion of the Gentiles, the outsiders, how much more will their full inclusion mean? If their rejection means the reconciliation of the world, what will their acceptance mean but life from the dead? Again, we note the transformative power of the proclamation of resurrection.

This leads Paul to two metaphors. First, he suggests that if part of the dough offered as first fruit is holy, then the whole batch will be holy. The metaphor of the first fruits and the leavened dough picks up imagery from Numbers 15:17–21 and Leviticus 19:23–25, another example of Paul in conversation with ancient Scripture to make sense of the present time. The first fruits correspond to the remnant of Jewish Christians, a part of the whole of Israel, the remnant sanctifying the totality. This metaphor, however, is apparently insufficient. Paul adds a second metaphor to develop more fully a description of the organic, dynamic interdependence of Jewish and Gentile communities within God's plan and to point toward the most hopeful end of the chapter.

The Metaphor of the Olive Tree
(Romans 11:17–24)

This second metaphor of the olive tree describes some branches broken off and others grafted in. Paul is echoing images found in the Hebrew Scriptures that speak of Israel as a tree.

> The Lord once called you, "A green olive tree, fair with goodly fruit"; but with the roar of a great tempest he will set fire to it and its branches will be consumed. (Jer. 11:16)

> His shoots shall spread out; his beauty shall be like the olive tree, and his fragrance like that of Lebanon. (Hos. 14:6)

The root and branches represent Paul's vision of Israel's ongoing participation in the unfolding mystery of God's purposes. Roots represent tradition, history, the patriarchs, the recipients of the promise, having a sanctifying effect on the whole tree.

To Gentiles he says: don't presume on the fact that you have been brought into community. He claims that Gentile Christianity must humbly recognize roots in the traditions reflected in the Hebrew Scriptures, that there is no hope for them apart from the history of Israel, that they are indeed dependent on that history. Gentiles are not to look down on Israel or presume an advantage over Israel, an attitude that would threaten the unity of the church, which may have already begun to take place. There is no grounds for boasting, and if there is any claim to be made, it would simply be one of dependence on the good news of grace, on the power of the promises of God (Rom. 3:2ff). As Paul says in 1 Corinthians 1:31: "Let the one who boasts, boast in the Lord." This verse is really a citation of Jeremiah 9:23–24: "Thus says the LORD: Do not let the wise boast in their wisdom, do not let the mighty boast in their might, do not let the wealthy boast in their wealth, but let those who boast boast in this, that they understand and know me, that I am the LORD; I act with steadfast love, justice and righteousness in the earth, for in these things I delight, says the LORD." The Gentile community has indeed been grafted into this community, but that is not an indication of any divine preference for them, nor a mark of rejection of past covenant. Gentiles have been included on the basis of grace, of faith. The only appropriate human response is to stand in awe, and for the two groups to live with each other in a spirit of humility and gratitude. Boasting is to be rejected because it signals the end of the faith in grace, the principle of inclusion.

In the beginning of the book, we read that the righteousness of God has been revealed both in God's wrath and in God's justification or right-wising. Here Paul phrases it differently, reminding the Romans of the kindness and severity of God, a counterpoint to the grace and wrath of God. Out of the tension of these two dynamics comes the possibility of resurrection, the power that all can be grafted into the living tree. The hardening process, the obduracy described in vv. 7–10, need not be the last word. The Gentiles disregard Israel at their peril. The people of Israel are the recipients of promises to which God will ultimately be faithful.

This metaphor of tree with branches coming and going defies natural grafting techniques, which doesn't seem to worry the apostle.

Paul does not present a new tree, as if the Christian community was a new entity, a new community, or a new race. He places the church in continuity with, and in dependence on, those who have received the promise.

His overriding concern is the unity of the community. As he warned against Jewish boasting in 3:27, in 11:15 he now argues against Gentile boasting. Any hint of human distinction and merit threatens the unity of the church as it rejects the gospel of grace and embraces the idolatrous notion that God somehow stands in debt to humanity. The unity of the church, the marvel, the mystery, the secret of these communities coming together, is essential to Paul as a witness to the coming glory of God. For the Christians addressed in the Letter to the Romans (as distinct from Christians addressed in the letter to the Galatians), the unity is achieved when the law is properly understood. The church emerges as a living witness to the ratification of God's promises. This fulfillment of the divine promise is to be realized in the unequivocal statement: The gifts and call of God are irrevocable.

All Israel Will Be Saved
(Romans 11:25–36)

Paul builds on the metaphor of the olive tree in such a way that it concludes as a message of hope for Israel. He began the chapter with a question: Has God rejected his people? Has God given up or gone away?

Again, as a way to guard against the boasting that is so destructive of human community, Paul describes a mystery, a secret now revealed, so that his readers will not claim to be wiser than they are, so that they can practice that rare Christian virtue of humility. At the end of the first eleven chapters, and especially at the end of these three chapters with complicated, sometimes convoluted argument, Paul brings this discussion to a conclusion that sums up the gospel.

All boasting from Gentiles about Jewish members of the community is to be set aside. The hardening, the obduracy of Israel is part of God's elective purpose. Indeed, as Richard Hays has noted, Israel undergoes rejection for the sake of the world, bearing suffering vicariously.[39] Rejection certainly is not the last word. That experience has opened the door for inclusion of Gentiles in the community of faith. In verses 25–32, Paul will sum up this argument with a concluding statement of his gospel, an explication of the mystery of God's purposes alluded to in vv. 12, 15, and 17–24.

It's a mystery that points to the process by which God's merciful purposes will be realized. First, a hardening has come on Israel so that the fullness of Gentiles may come into the church. That fullness (*pleroma*) of Gentiles in turn anticipates the salvation of all of Israel.

Paul is not explicit about what all Israel means, whether it is the totality of those who are Jewish by birth, or a group known to God—actually the group that God foreknew. The theme of universality that pervades the whole letter, beginning with the statement in 3:9 that all are under the power of sin, is now expressed here as inclusion for all.

Entering into conversation with his own Scriptures, Paul cites several passages from Isaiah (59:20–21a and 27:9) to note that this salvation will come as an experience of deliverance and forgiveness, focusing the action on God's initiative. One can understand why Paul refers to this as mystery, for he describes Israel at once as being the enemies of God for the sake of the Gentiles, as well as beloved of God for the sake of their ancestors, based on the faithfulness of God. But if it is mysterious, it is also unequivocal. God will not go back on God's gifts. The gifts and call of God are irrevocable, a reprise of the affirmation that nothing can separate from the love of God.

It's a mystery indeed, because Paul has on the one hand affirmed the incontrovertible will of God. At the same time, he holds out the possibility that some will be ungrafted from the root (Rom. 11:22). There appears to be a place for human initiative, a call to continue in God's kindness (Rom. 2:4) echoed in Paul's warning that we must take heed lest we fall (1 Cor. 10:12) that sounds very much like human possibility. The analogy unfolded in Romans 11:17–24 suggests that faith can be lost. In contrast, v. 29 suggests that grace is the final word, a power that overcomes unbelief, irresistibly calling into existence that which does not exist (Rom. 4:17f)

It's a mystery that will be revealed in days to come. The tension between enemy and beloved, the resolution to the contradiction posed by God's faithfulness and human responsibility rest in the future orientation of these verses which conclude this section and bring Paul's argument to climax. Nothing will confound God's victory. Nothing will ultimately separate us from God, not even unbelief. In the present that tension is not completely or apparently resolved. It cannot be easily understood. It may simply call for faith, for trust. The irrevocable call and gifts are not to be confused with complacency, license, or grounds for boasting. Life in the church is to be marked by continued life in God's kindness. It is not as a matter of merit but as a witness to the future demonstration of God's kindness.

Life in the church is to be marked by continued life in God's kindness.

It's a mystery by which the status of those described as enemies of God is superseded by God's freedom to show mercy. The unbelief of those with whom Paul contends will not invalidate the faithfulness of God. In an interweaving of Jewish and Gentile experience, Paul sees all of humanity in the same place. God has imprisoned all in disobedience so that God may be merciful to all.

The end of the story, the end of the road, the end of Paul's argument is mercy toward all, an answer to the question in 9:16. Divine consignment, seen in the beginning of the letter in 1:24, 26, 28 where God hands over objects of wrath to the consequences of their actions, is countered by the divine intention to show mercy, a theme that Paul also strikes in the Letter to the Galatians, which says that the Scripture consigned all things to sin, so that what was promised to faith in Jesus Christ might be given to those who believe.

Mercy is God's ultimate word to humanity. Thus mercy, this divine disposition, constitutes its hope. Mercy, a term used repeatedly in this section of the letter (9:15, 16, 18, 23; 11:30–32; 12:8; 15:9), sums up the gospel of the justification of the ungodly. Grace, a power that administers mercy, breaks into the sphere of wrath. The gospel emerges out of disobedience. All have been imprisoned. All have been shown mercy. This is the gospel of which Paul is not ashamed.

In the end, Paul may or may not have been successful in crafting a compelling argument for his readers, either in the first century or in ours. But his confidence that the final word for all will be a word of mercy leads him to set aside argument and explanation. Instead, he breaks into a song of adoration, a hymn of praise, which is often where we are left. Perhaps it is not unlike the conclusion of Job, who after all the hard questions that book poses about the faithfulness of God, comes to recognize that it is indeed a mystery beyond human understanding.

In the End, It All Comes Down to Worship (Romans 11:33–36)

Worship has been a theme throughout the letter. The universality of sin has been described as the tendency of all people to resort to idolatry, to be misguided in worship, to give one's heart to that which will not satisfy one's heart. At the end of the eleventh chapter, Paul witnesses to the quality of mercy by which God's character is revealed, so that it can be seen that God is faithful. God is in control. God is merciful.

All of the tensions have not been logically explained, for sure. We live in and with mystery. Nevertheless, there is an unequivocal affirmation that mercy will win out, a variation of the theme that the arc of history is long but it bends toward justice. Paul speaks of the unsearchable judgments, the inscrutable ways of God, entering into conversation with his own selections from Scripture which point to the transcendent wisdom and self-sufficiency of God. He cites Scriptures from Isaiah and pointedly brings in a reference from Job, which in many ways tackles themes similar to the questions raised by the Letter to the Romans and ends in a similar place.

As in other places in the letter (1:25, 9:5, 16:25–27), these three chapters end with doxology, an affirmation that the whole process of salvation is due to God's initiative, a process that remains in God's control from beginning to end. Our conversation with Scripture and especially with Paul's meandering arguments, marked by detours and mixed metaphors, might lead us to imagine that Paul has given up at the dead end of an argument. But this hymn indicates that worship is the proper human response to divine initiative. "In his prayer of praise, Paul asserts the infinite distance between human knowledge and God's action."[40] The theme of the epistle that God is the only proper object of worship, an argument against idolatry, is restated.

In chapters 12–15, Paul will show what that worship means for the church as well as the nature of true spiritual worship, in the community and in the world—worship offered with our lips and with our lives. In this way, chapters 9–11 have served as a bridge between chapters 1–8 and the concluding chapters of the epistle. Rather than functioning as a digression or detour, these three chapters have proved to be an integral passage in the letter. They state the mystery of the gospel in such a way that it truly becomes good news for all. The affirmations of God's faithfulness (in the irrevocable gifts and call) and God's sovereignty (in consigning all to disobedience and ultimately to mercy) lead to a response of praise, for Romans 9–11 has been, according to Richard Hays, an "extended demonstration of the congruity between God's word in Scripture and God's word in Paul's gospel."[41]

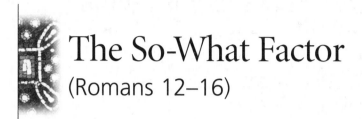

## CHAPTER SEVEN

The So-What Factor
(Romans 12–16)

> *If I were a nightingale I would do what*
> *is proper to a nightingale, but in fact I am*
> *a rational creature, so I must praise God.*
>
> —EPICTETUS, *DISCOURSES,* I VXI. 20FF.)

A seminary professor guided our class through study of several New Testament books, inviting students to take turns making presentations on assigned passages. Though I took the class a number of years ago, the simplicity of his approach has stayed with me in conversation with Scripture in parish life, in preaching, and in my own journey of faith. He encouraged us to ask this series of questions: When (was it written)? Who (wrote and received it)? Why (was it written, and written the way it was)? How (is the case made)? What (does the text say)?

Out of all these questions, the most important was the final one: So what? What difference does this passage make? How did it shape the ways that the community which heard the text put faith to work in the world? More to the point, how does it shape the way we put faith to work in the world? Where does it intersect with our lives? What does it call us to do and be?

The final section of the Letter to the Romans covers the last five chapters. In preceding chapters, Paul has argued for an expansive view of God's grace, a universal demonstration of mercy affirming the faithfulness of God to

Dogmatic teaching reflects the dogma or doctrine of the church, and does not necessarily connote some of the negative associations that suggest obstinant or rigid religious thinking.

promises made over the centuries. The righteousness of God shapes a community in which all are welcome, a community characterized by unity. In this final section, Paul challenges his readers to put that faith to work in the world, with particular focus on the character of community life. The section is filled with practical directives.

As such, it may seem distinct from the theological argument that has preceded it. But the continuity is strong. As C. K. Barrett notes: "The dogmatic teaching is misunderstood if it is not seen to require ethical action, and the ethical teaching cannot be grasped if it is not recognized that it rests at every point upon the dogmatics."[42]

The Transformed Life (Romans 12:1–8)

Our conversation with Paul's letter has focused on the transforming effect, the power *(dunamis)* of God's grace. That focus is reflected in the first eight verses of chapter 12. Paul begins with the word "Therefore" (again leading us to ask what the "therefore" is there for), an indication that what will follow comes in response to God's grace. He points to the synergy of God's initiative and human response, captured in the theme of worship. A faithful human response comes as a response to all that has been stated in chapters 1–11, a response to the mercies of God. In this way, as Cranfield says, "All truly Christian moral endeavor is theocentric, having its origin not in a humanistic desire for the enhancement of the self by the attainment of moral superiority nor in the legalist's illusory hope of putting God under obligation, but simply in the gracious action of God."[43]

Paul appeals to the congregation in Rome; indeed as one translation puts it, he beseeches them to present themselves a living sacrifice (v. 1, NRSV). In language that can be helpful in contemporary conversation regarding atonement theories, in contrast to killing something as a sacrifice, Paul calls for a living offering, holy and well pleasing, made possible by the mercies of God. Paul frames this response as spiritual worship. The King James Version renders the phrase "spiritual worship" as "reasonable service," an expression of worship that consists not in outward ritual but in the movement of the inner being, the movement of the heart.

What will that praise look like? We hear echoes of the Hebrew Scripture in the call to worship. Psalm 50:24 speaks about the kind of sacrifice God desires, an offering of thanksgiving. Deuteronomy 6:5 says that the worship God desires pertains to the love of God with heart, soul, and mind. Elsewhere in the New Testament, a related passage in 1 Peter 2:2–5 calls early Christians to let themselves be "built into a spiritual house, to be a holy priesthood, to offer spiritual sacrifices acceptable to God through Jesus Christ." As we noted in the end of chapter 11, it's all about worship, righteousness rightly understood as right relationship with God, which in turn gets expressed in right relationship with the community and the world.

Paul sets up a contrast, an echo of his discussion of the contrast of spirit and flesh in chapter 5. He calls on readers not to be conformed to this age, but to be transformed (in the Greek, *metamorphousthai*) so that they can experience the resurrected life of grace that has blasted (like dynamite) through old patterns of human behavior, breaking down old divisions, overcoming obstacles that constrain healed relationships. Paul envisions radical renewal, an old age fading away, a new age emerging, manifested in the life of the members of the community. It is a call to a new way of life, turning from the way of life described in the first chapter, made possible through baptism described in the sixth chapter (a dying to the old, a rising to the new). We now see how that new way of life occurs, how it will be a witness to the world. The renewal of the mind, the effect of baptism (see Titus 3:5), understood as gift, grace, or sacrament is something that God empowers.

That new life will be evident to the world through the witness of the unity of the church. People who had formerly been separated are brought together in one communion. Boasting about who is better or more righteous will be dismissed. This eschatological ethic, which is to say, an ethic for an emerging age, will result from a renewed way of regarding God, the one who meets us with grace prior to anything we do. It will lead to a renewed way of regarding each other, freed from divisive pretense of boasting. Acting as spiritual coach, Paul proceeds in the final chapters to describe what that life of renewal looks like.

To accomplish that task Paul relies on a metaphor for the church that was used in antiquity to describe the political body. The Roman historian Livy used the metaphor of the body, for example, to argue that the Senate and the Roman people could no more dispense with each other than the stomach and limbs could do without one another. They formed a unity within one body.[44]

Similarly, in the Letter to the Romans and elsewhere Paul has used the metaphor in appeal to the church. Members of the body should not think more highly of themselves. In yet another call to put boasting aside, he suggests that in the community there were people who were falling into this way of thinking. The community is called to sobermindedness, a virtue indicating soundness of mind, prudence, discretion, and moderation, mindful of the ways that God has provided measure of faith. Note one more time Paul's conviction that this is God's work, and that a person who is humble before God is less likely to be arrogant in relationship to fellow creatures.

The metaphor of the body of Christ teaches about diversity in unity. Thanks be to God, unity is not uniformity. In the life of the community that follows Jesus, members have different functions, all necessary for the proper working of the body, with no occasion for any to think too highly of himself or herself, no room for groups in the community to claim that they are better than other groups. It is an idea presented at length in 1 Corinthians 12:12–31, where Paul speaks about the body of Christ. In imagery that is about as humorous as he gets (which is not all that humorous), Paul talks about how no part of the body is indispensable. No part can say to another part that they don't need each other. Distinctive gifts (in Greek, *charisma*) in the community are not intended to indicate human distinction, accomplishment, or hierarchy. Rather, they are gifts of grace, apportioned according to God's grace, intended for edification, for the building up of the body.

The gifts that are listed in Romans 12 include prophecy, the communication of God's word in inspired and intelligible speech (see 1 Cor. 12 and 14); ministry (*diakonia* from which we derive the word "deacon"), which suggests service and, perhaps in a more focused way, service to those in need; and teaching, the task of unpacking truth, which could also be the ministry of a preacher, the communication of the gospel to the hearer, something that Paul has described as indispensable in Romans 9. An exhorter carries out similar ministry, as leader in the community functioning as spiritual coach. The giver is identified with the gift of generosity. The one who presides, perhaps a technical term for an office holder, is to do so with zeal. It's not clear, and perhaps intentionally so, whether this indicates presiding at a liturgy or presiding at a meeting or deliberative event. Both can be spiritual experiences. Both can be occasions for responding to grace. (Would that many of our church meetings knew that zeal in their leadership.) The one who is given the gift of compassion is called to express that gift with cheerfulness.

What would our churches look like if we were to discover a spiritually vibrant response to the grace of God by allowing these different gifts to find full expression? How would our communities be transformed if they existed without competition and celebrated the good news that in our diversity we are all united. We are one. We are all on the receiving end of a profound mercy. At the end of this book, we will pose questions about where you see these gifts at work in the community in which you serve.

What Does the Christian Life Look Like?
(Romans 12:9–21)

Paul puts one of these spiritual gifts to work in this passage, the spiritual gift of exhortation. He coaches this congregation in what it means to be a community reflecting the transforming power of grace. Just as grace is presented as unconditional favor extended to human beings by God, so the community is to reflect that same kind of favor in its common life and in the world. Love is to be expressed as genuine. It is especially expressed in hospitality, a virtue in the early church, mentioned again in Romans 16:1–2, but also in Hebrews 13:2 ("Do not neglect to show hospitality to strangers, for by doing that some have entertained angels without knowing it"). That spirit of hospitality is carried on in the tradition through the Rule of St. Benedict, which says that the stranger is to be welcomed as Christ.[45]

While we have noted that the death and resurrection of Jesus seem to be the primary Christological concern throughout Paul's letters, Paul appears mindful of the teaching of Jesus as he counsels Roman Christians on what it means to put faith to work in the world. While Paul rarely quotes Jesus directly, this twelfth chapter of Romans echoes ethical injunctions from the Sermon on the Mount, specifically Matthew 5:38–42 where Jesus instructs disciples not to return evil for evil, but to overcome evil with good as part of an ethic signaling a new age. Paul echoes Matthew 5:9 when he calls the Roman Christians to live at peace with all.

As part of his ongoing conversation with the Scriptures of his tradition, Paul also echoes Deuteronomy 32:35 when he tells the congregation to resist taking vengeance into their own hands. If the reader is troubled by the manipulative suggestion that kindness will heap coals upon an enemy's head, it may help to recognize that Paul is reprising both Deuteronomy and Proverbs 25:21–22, applying them to his own time.

The Christian's Life in the Empire (Romans 13:1–7)

Then, as if he were writing to a Christian community in Washington, DC, or another modern center of political power, Paul describes the ways that Christians should comport themselves in relationship to political authorities. Paul explores the relationship of the church and political authority, reminding us that there are a variety of perspectives within Scripture addressing this relationship.

In fact, there are a number of perspectives within writings attributed to Paul. On the one hand, this passage is similar to other New Testament affirmations (1 Pet. 2:13–17, with a call to fear God and honor the emperor). At the same time, this passage stands in contrast to other writings (for instance, 1 Cor. 2:6–8, 15:24–26; 1 Thess. 5:3–11) where Paul asserts that the Christian community must contend with the principalities and powers of the age. This exhortation in Romans 13 stands in contrast to his own willingness to contest civil authorities (2 Cor. 11:23, 25–27), and perhaps contradicts the beginning of this chapter, which speaks about not being conformed to this world. It marks a contrast to the ways that other apostles related to civil authorities—for instance, Acts 5:29 where Peter says: "We must obey God rather than any human authority."

All of this points us to the way that Paul does theology. His thinking is contingent, flexible, responding to the particularity of a given situation. Said another way, Paul doesn't always do what he always does. As he says in 1 Corinthians, he becomes all things to all people. These verses may well emerge from the contingent experience of this community gathered in Rome, by which Paul is trying to show that he is not promoting rebellion against the empire. (He was already in enough trouble.) In our own conversation with Scripture, and in our own reading of history, in fact, in the reading of the daily news, we readily note exceptions to Paul's claim in verse 3 that "rulers are not a terror to good conduct, but to bad." Paul's teaching on paying taxes echoes Jesus teaching about the Roman tribute, found in the synoptic gospels (Matt. 22:21, Mark 12:17, Luke 20:25), although one is put in mind of Dorothy Day's reputed comment when she said that if we rendered to God the things that are God's, there would be little left over for Caesar.

Here, Paul offers a vision of civil authorities ordained by God. Perhaps Paul was thinking about Cyrus, the Persian ruler who in the Hebrew Scriptures is referred to as a messiah (Isaiah 45:1, see also Ezra 1:1) because of his instrumentality in helping Israel return from exile. Paul asserts that to resist divinely ordained authority is to incur judgment.

We do not know the particular context here for Paul or for the community he addressed. We do recognize that the witness of Scripture, and particularly the story of the early church, presents a varied, maybe even an ambivalent picture of the relationship of early Christians to civil authorities.

Throughout the history of the church, the Christian community has celebrated those who resist authority and who practice civil disobedience for the sake of justice and peace. We are left with plenty of room for conversation with Scripture, as we explore tensions between citizenship on earth and citizenship in heaven, as we explore what it means for Christians living in a system that aspires to participatory democracy to live faithfully as disciples and citizens, and as we strive to be stewards of the freedoms we enjoy.

What's Love Got to Do with It?
(Romans 13:8–14)

Paul writes: "Owe no one anything, except to love one another; for the one who loves another has fulfilled the law" (v. 8). In this passage, Paul picks up a theme presented several times in this letter (2:14, 8:4, 12:9) and in other letters (e.g., Gal. 4:4). It also echoes what Jesus said in the gospels about the ways that love of God and love of neighbor fulfill the law (Matt. 22:39–40; Mark 12:31). Here, we also find a "deliberate echo of Romans 10:4: "For Christ is the end of the law so that there may be righteousness for everyone who believes."[46] Even the Letter of James in the New Testament, often seen as counterpoint to Paul's teaching, conveys the same message.

The ethic that Paul espouses here is predicated on the imminent expectation of Christ's coming, the conviction that a new age has dawned with the death and resurrection of Jesus. Paul uses language found in apocalyptic sections of the gospels, language associated with the season of Advent, a season of expectation. He speaks of the need to be awake, to look for approaching salvation, to recognize that the dawn is breaking. It is time to put on the armor of light, an ethic expressed in 1 Thessalonians (especially chapter 5), the earliest of the letters, one in which the return of Jesus was expected quite soon.

As time went on, with the delay of Christ's return, it became clear that the Lord's appearance would come in ways that were unexpected or surprising. In contemporary conversation with Scripture, as we translate Paul's context to our own, how do our ethics shift as we acknowledge that Christ's return has not happened in the ways that Paul may have expected?

We make this affirmation in our Eucharistic prayer: Christ has died, Christ has risen, Christ will come again. How does that affirmation shape our way of life in the world, a life marked by the expectancy of that arrival? Our liturgical calendar, beginning the year with the season of Advent, draws us into themes of expectancy, calls us to be awake, to be alert, to be ready, to live in expectation of God's future redemptive activity. As we ask questions about our individual journeys of faith and the lives of our communities of faith, we continue to read in Paul's letter about this ethic of expectation and hope, and how it transforms a community.

That kind of transformation is simply captured in Paul's injunction: "Put on the Lord Jesus Christ." This imagery is associated with baptism. In the early church, before candidates for baptism were immersed in the water, they were stripped of their clothes. After emerging from the water, new white clothes were put on them. All of that ritual symbolized the new way of life to which the community was called.

Life in Community: The Strong and the Weak (Romans 14:1–12)

That transformed community will exhibit a spirit of love, the fulfillment of the great commandment in specific ways. Love God and love neighbor. It's a simple command, if not an easy one.

Paul recognizes the diversity of this Roman congregation, comprised of Jewish Christians who adhere to the observance of certain traditions about diet and special days. One can infer that Gentile Christians, described as stronger in faith, did not recognize these observances. In Paul's mind, those who are stronger in the faith are those who seem less tied to rules and regulations. Those who are weaker in the faith are those whose spiritual life hinges on the observance of those rules.

That may run counter to our impressions of spiritual strength. A more intense religious observance is often equated with spiritual strength. A fruitful area for conversation comes in asking what it means to be strong in faith, and what it means to be weak. How does that relate to Paul's claim in 2 Corinthians 12:9, where Paul says that God's grace is sufficient because God's strength is made perfect in weakness?

Apparently, in the community, the difference in observance was causing conflict. The higher call for the community, to be repeated again, is one of welcome. "Welcome those who are weak in faith,"

There is to be a spirit not simply of tolerance or inclusion, but honor and respect. It is not about who is right. It is about appreciating the different ways that people feel called to honor their Lord, the different ways that people feel called to express their gratitude to God, the different ways people feel called to worship.

Paul says. That does not mean agreement or uniformity. It is a celebration of the dignity of difference. There is to be a spirit not simply of tolerance or inclusion, but honor and respect. It is not about who is right. It is about appreciating the different ways that people feel called to honor their Lord, the different ways that people feel called to express their gratitude to God, the different ways people feel called to worship. Implicit in this reference to the divisions that emerge because of differences in the community is the concern that Paul has about boasting.

In language that has been incorporated into the anthems that open the Burial Office in the Book of Common Prayer. Paul says that we do not live or die to ourselves, and that our life and our death belong to the Lord, continuing the theme in chapter 6 by which baptism is seen as a way of dying to the old life, dying to the old self. With that in mind, Paul calls on the members of the community in Rome to avoid judging others. Such judgment is predicated on that spirit of boasting, creating toxic divisions in the community and harming the witness of the church to the world.

Walking in Love (Romans 14:13–23)

Paul offers specific examples of what a community transformed by grace looks like. It is a community of righteousness, a matter of being in right relationship with each other. That community will be marked by a willingness to forgo one's own agenda for the better of another, most definitely a countercultural thing to do. It's a variation on the theme of renouncing boasting, which is all about that ego which seeks to "edge God out." Paul calls on members of the community to stop judging each other, to avoid those things that get in the way of spiritual growth, the spiritual transformation of the other. It is a radical vision of community focused on servanthood.

Paul is often presented as someone who liked to lay down a lot of rules. He often comes through that way when only excerpts of his letters surface in the lectionary. Truth be told, he offers a different ethic.

In a sign of his own radical departure from the tradition in which he was raised, a sign of his own change, his own transformation, he admits that nothing is unclean in and of itself, an affirmation of the goodness of creation, a witness to original blessing.

As he presumably responds to division in the congregation to which he writes, he says that specific religious observance is not the issue. The issue is whether a church member is injuring another by the freedom, perhaps even the license that member enjoys. The highest end to be pursued is that which makes for peace and mutual up-building. Edification, critical to the unity of the church to which Paul is committed, is threatened by disputes about food.

Edification results from the surrender of ego, a spirit of humility. His call to this community finds another expression in 1 Corinthians 13, where Paul talks to a divided community, noting various gifts in the community, claiming that they mean nothing if love is not active. In that passage, he says love "bears all things, believes all things, hopes all things, endures all things" (13:7). Later on, in that same letter (1 Cor, 14:3–5, 12, 26), Paul speaks of the ultimate goal of edification. Whatever a member of the community does, it must spring from an attitude marked by faith, by conviction. The Christian community is to be marked by a spirit that honors the other.

The Strong Bear the Burdens of the Weak
(Romans 15:1–13)

As Paul concludes this letter, he addresses the community with a call for the strong to put up with failings of the weak, to put aside the pleasing of self. Christ provides the model of discipleship, the one who came not to be served but to serve (Mark 10:45), not pleasing himself but willingly taking on insults. Paul addresses these disciples of Christ, calling on members of this community to welcome each other as Christ has welcomed them. In many ways, that is yet another succinct summation of his argument in this letter.

Divine initiative has come in Christ welcoming humanity into relationship, a graceful event, an original blessing. In response, that welcome is to be extended by members of the community, as an expression of faith, offered to the glory of God, offered as worship.

Paul sums up the letter with a vision of Christ as a servant of the circumcised, confirming promises made to the patriarchs so that the Gentiles might experience the glory of God as well. In keeping with the approach that has guided Paul in writing this letter and with his own conversation with Scripture, he includes a collection of quotations from the Psalms, Deuteronomy, and Isaiah, all as an indication that what he is saying is hardly new.

Closing Arguments (Romans 15:14–33)

As Paul began the letter with a warm greeting to a congregation that he did not know (1:8, 11–12), he concludes by echoing the affirmation of those first verses, describing a congregation of people filled with goodness, with knowledge, and with the ability to instruct each other.

He admits that he has spoken boldly. The boldness to which he refers may have to do with the radical notion that the Gentiles are full members of the body of Christ. He has done so as a minister of Christ Jesus to the Gentiles (13:6), functioning not only as a public servant, but in a priestly role.[47] His is a ministry directed to the Gentiles as in 11:13 and Galatians 2:9, where the Jewish leadership of the church affirms his call to preach to the Gentiles. It is an echo of the living sacrifice he has spoken about in the beginning of chapter 12, as he sees himself set apart in a priestly ministry. It brings to mind the call of the priest in the ordination service in the Book of Common Prayer in which the priest is instructed by the bishop to nourish Christ's people from the riches of God's grace.[48] That liturgy confirms what Paul says, that it is not the human activity of the priest that offers nourishment, but the grace of God. Paul envisions that kind of instrumentality for his own ministry with this congregation.

In a letter that has consistently spoken about the perils of boasting, Paul continues by saying in verse 17 that in Christ Jesus he has reason for boasting. By grace, Christ has worked through him to incorporate Gentiles into the community of faith, a work of the spirit of God, a work animated by signs and wonders. He repeats his intention to take the gospel to places where it has not been preached, to share the news of grace that has such power to transform relationships.

He talks about his own missionary strategy, focused on new territory. He has preached the gospel in Jerusalem (though Acts 9:29 indicates that it was not particularly well-received) and as far around as Illyricum. His goal is to proclaim the good news to places where Christ "has not been named," lest he build on someone else's foundation.

At this late stage in the letter he adds a metaphor for his work (a metaphor that he also uses in 1 Corinthians) as he discusses the importance of building on the proper foundation, which in his mind is Jesus Christ. He sees his work as part of the construction of a new temple. His commission, his call to ministry fulfills prophecy in Isaiah 52:6–15, which says that those who have never been told will see and will understand. The passage is a counterbalance to the perplexing verses from Isaiah 6:9–10 cited earlier in the book and which appear in many places in the New Testament, which is an effort to understand why many do not embrace the gospel he proclaims.

One might ask why, if Paul sees himself as a trailblazer, he intends to visit Rome, since someone else has obviously already started building the church there. In verses 22–33, Paul speaks with specificity about his plans, noting that he desires to come to them on his way to Spain, a place that has not yet heard the gospel of grace. First he will go to Jerusalem, bringing resources that churches in Macedonia and Achaia have offered, sharing not only spiritual blessings but also material blessings for the sake of those in need in Jerusalem. Paul wishes first to deliver these expressions of support (see 1 Cor. 16:1–5; 2 Cor. 8), a ministry to the poor among the saints in Jerusalem. This collection with its sacramental dimension is an outward and visible sign of the unity of Christ, and it points to the interconnectedness of these communities. It provides us with an image of the body of Christ. It suggests all kinds of possibilities for the global church today.

Paul appeals to the congregation again, asking that they will pray for him, that he will be rescued from unbelievers in Judea, that his ministry might be acceptable to the saints, that he might come to them with joy. The book of Acts does indeed speak about Paul making his way to Rome after the trip to Jerusalem, but it was not the way he intended to show up.

The account in Acts has Paul traveling to Rome as a prisoner. Paul apparently was not able to get to Spain. Tradition has it that he arrives in Rome, spends time as a house prisoner, and is eventually martyred there.

Commendation and Greetings
(Romans 16:1–23)

It sounds as if the end of chapter 15, which ends with the prayer that "the God of peace be with all of you," could mark the end of the letter. Some early manuscripts omit this last chapter. Some scholars doubt whether Paul would have known so many people in a community he had never visited. But as the letter has been passed on, it includes this chapter chocked full of specific greetings, with the mention of many names, offering insights into the character and composition of the community in Rome. These specific notes anchor this letter in a specific context, when at times it may seem like theological argument removes the conversation from congregational life.

We meet Phoebe, a deacon of the church of Cenchreae, the eastern port of Corinth, commended to this community to be welcomed as one of the saints, someone who has been a benefactor for Paul and others.[49] Paul lists other members of the Roman congregation (we won't mention them all), including Prisca and Aquila, identified in Acts 18 as exiles from Rome in a simple but chilling line which speaks about how Jews were required to leave Rome (Acts 18:2). That would explain how these two ended up in Corinth, where they helped Paul establish a church, working alongside him in bivocational ministry. If indeed this letter was written after the death of Claudius (in October of 54 CE), they may have returned to Rome when the persecution of Jews was eased. They are also mentioned in 1 Corinthians 16:19. All of those who met in their house are greeted, an insight in how the first Christians gathered.

Paul greets people who get little or no other mention in the New Testament. Of particular interest in this list are references to beloved Epaenetus, the first convert in Asia for Christ (Rom 16:5; 1 Cor.

16:15). There is a reference to Andronicus and Junia, fellow prisoners (relatives or compatriots) with Paul who were prominent among the apostles. Junia is in some places translated Julia, a woman's name. Many manuscripts read Junias, a male Latin name, with the suggestion that in the transmission of these texts, there was an agenda aimed at removal of references to women in leadership roles.

It is notable that in this list there are a number of women apparently serving in leadership roles. When Paul refers to these persons as relatives, it may be an indication that they were Jewish brothers or sisters. We see here that the term "apostle" refers to a group wider than the twelve disciples (1 Cor. 15:5, 7). In Philippians 2:25, Paul refers to his colleague Epaphroditus as someone sent as a messenger, in the Greek, *apostolon,* from which we get the English word apostle

Rufus, an outstanding or elect Christian, is mentioned. There may be a connection to Rufus who is the son of Simon of Cyrene, the one who carried Jesus's cross and may have been known in the community for which Mark's gospel was written.

In the midst of greeting, Paul cannot resist one more dose of spiritual coaching. So there comes a warning, an echo that the unity of the church is of great concern, a matter of importance for the sake of the witness to the world. Paul is mindful of those who would cause dissensions and offenses, perhaps a reference to those involved in judging and boasting, leading to distinction between groups.

The section of personal greetings concludes with specific people who extend greetings to the Roman congregation, many of them names familiar to those who have traced the journeys of Paul.[50] All of this indicates that while Paul has never visited this congregation, there are connections that have formed as the body of Christ has grown beyond local congregation, and as these various congregations are led to deeper interconnectedness and mutual responsibility as the body of Christ.

A Benediction (Romans 16:25–27)

The letter closes with a benediction or a blessing which appears in different manuscripts at different places. It is entirely absent from some manuscripts, and it may have been added by later scribes or editors. It uses language associated with later texts, similar in part to Ephesians 3:20–21, 1 Timothy 1:17, and Jude 24–25. Whether the blessing comes from Paul's hand or not, it summarizes themes of the gospel in a doxology, underscoring the message that this whole letter is about worshipping the God whose initiative of grace has reached out in new ways. This hymn is offered in praise of the God who offers strength, mediated or revealed through the proclamation of the gospel of Jesus Christ. For Paul, Jesus Christ marks the advent of a new age, a revelation of a mystery that has not previously been disclosed but is now unveiled, a secret that has universal effect, as all are invited into the experience of God's grace.

## CHAPTER EIGHT

Conclusion

We conclude our conversation with this letter, mindful of the many levels of conversation that have taken place, knowing that we have just scratched the surface. Those varied exchanges include the conversation between Paul and a congregation he had not met, a conversation within the community, taking place between different groups, between Jews and Gentiles, between those who are strong and weak. It is also a conversation with the tradition, with the sacred texts of Israel, the Hebrew Scriptures, and with the culture of the day, especially the culture of the Roman Empire's capital.

In their own way, each of these conversations explores questions about God's character as revealed in the story of Jesus. Paul speaks of the ways that the righteousness and the faithfulness of God have been manifested. He has celebrated the gospel of grace as a transforming event.

Each of these conversations explores questions about what it means to be part of the community that follows Jesus, or in Paul's language, the body of Christ. The proclamation at the heart of the letter holds the promise of a transforming reality. Our conversation with this portion of

Scripture matters because that transforming reality can still take place in the lives of individuals, and in our congregations.

That call to change is reflected in the liturgy of the Episcopal Church, notably in the General Thanksgiving found at the conclusion of the service of Morning Prayer:

> Almighty God, Father of all mercies, we your unworthy servants give you humble thanks for all your goodness and loving-kindness to us and to all whom you have made. We bless you for our creation, preservation, and all the blessings of this life; but above all for your immeasurable love in the redemption of the world by our Lord Jesus Christ; for the means of grace, and for the hope of glory. And, we pray, give us such an awareness of your mercies, that with truly thankful hearts we may show forth your praise, not only with our lips, but in our lives, by giving up ourselves to your service, and by walking before you in holiness and righteousness all our days; through Jesus Christ our Lord, to whom, with you and the Holy Spirit, be honor and glory throughout all ages. Amen.[51]

Did you notice how this prayer of thanksgiving, offered in the context of worship, follows the argument of Paul's Letter to the Romans? It describes the immeasurable love revealed to the world, the healing of the world offered through Jesus Christ, the means of grace and the hope of glory. The transforming power of that grace is unfolded in the request that the awareness of God's mercies would show forth our praise, not only with our lips but also in our lives.

In other words, this prayer is about the transforming power of grace. For Paul, it is the promise of transformation in the relationship between God and this congregation. It is also the promise of transformation in the lives of individuals in those communities. It is all about grace. So our conversation will conclude by recalling this reflection on the meaning of grace offered by Paul Tillich in his book *The Shaking of the Foundations* (cited earlier in this book, p. 6):

> Simply accept the fact that you are accepted. If that happens to us, we experience grace. After such an experience we may not be better than before, and we may not believe more than before. But everything is transformed. In that moment, grace conquers sin, and reconciliation bridges the gulf of estrangement. . . . In the light of this grace we perceive the power of grace in our relation to others and to ourselves.[52]

May God give us the grace to accept that we have been accepted. May we embrace that grace, so that the community that follows Jesus will be marked by a spirit of love, and will share that love with a world in deep need of the transforming power of grace.

ACKNOWLEDGMENTS

I give thanks for my teachers along the way. I'm grateful for biblical scholars who brought sacred text to life, and deepened my appreciation for the courageous ministry of St. Paul. I have in mind Dr. Joel Marcus, Dr. Louis Martyn, The Rev. Fleming Rutledge, Dr. Christopher Morse, Dr. Richard B. Hays, and Dr. Christiaan Beker. I'm grateful to Frederick Schmidt, Ryan Masteller, and Samantha Franklin who guided me through the editorial process. I'd also like to express gratitude to those who have taught me about transforming grace by example: Frances Murchison, my children, John Reid and Helen, my mother and grandmother, both named Grace, Scott Carlton, the Young Pups, and as the dedication indicates, John Murchison.

STUDY QUESTIONS

Chapter One

- How does change happen in the lives of individuals and in the lives of congregations and other communities?
- As you look in the spiritual rearview mirror, when has change happened in your spiritual journey?
- When has it taken place in the lives of communities to which you belong?
- Read the portion of Paul Tillich's sermon that talks about grace. If you are in a group, talk about how it informs your understanding of grace. How would you define grace?
- As you embark on the reading of Paul's letter, reflect on your own impressions of Paul. What do you know about him? What do you admire about him? What bothers you about him?

Chapter Two

- Paul is reaching out to this community, introducing himself and beginning to present his vision of the gospel. As you enter into conversation with Scripture, think about Paul's call to ministry in light of your own, in recognition that we are all ministers in the church. What does it mean in our world to be a servant? What does it mean to be an apostle? What does it mean to be a saint?
- Reflect on the words at the heart of Paul's thesis. How do you understand words like "gospel" and "salvation"? What, if any, meaning do they hold in our contemporary context? What

does it mean to speak of righteousness? Where have you seen it at work? Does the gospel have power? If so, where have you seen that power at work? If it has no power, why not? What does it mean to live by faith?

- Finally, spend some time in reflection on the thesis of this letter, presented in Romans 1:16–17. How would you complete this introductory phrase in such a way that it would reflect your understanding of the gospel: "I am not ashamed of the gospel, for it is . . ."

- Write your own thesis, your own mission statement that sums up your understanding of the gospel, the good news.

Chapter Three

- What kind of conversation is triggered by Scripture that speaks of the wrath of God? Does it make sense to begin a discussion of the power of the gospel with the language of judgment? Do we relegate this vision of God to a different time and place, to another cultural context, to a more primitive understanding of God, with a more fear-based religion?

- As you discuss this phrase, "the wrath of God," can it in any way be seen as part of the proclamation of the gospel? Can it be good news? Might it, for instance, be understood as the consequence, the experience of life without God, life without spirit, life without community, life divorced from covenant, life devoid of promise? What does that kind of life look like? What are the consequences of people buying into the notion that the universe centers around them?

- Language of wrath and judgment is present in numerous portions of the Hebrew Scripture, when both the people of Israel and their opponents experience divine judgment. Less commonly acknowledged are passages in the New Testament, specifically the ways that Jesus spoke of judgment, in a number of parables toward the end of Jesus's public ministry, in his own apocalyptic teaching. Note the judgment described in Matthew 25, where judgment comes to those who failed to feed the hungry and clothe the naked. In our liturgy, when we say the Nicene Creed, we affirm that the judgment of

Christ will be part of our future. How does that square with your vision of Jesus?

- If Scripture does indeed function as a mirror, where do we see ourselves in this passage? Who might be regarded as those bad people out there, people who exist beyond the reach of God's mercy? Who might be regarded as those folks who stand in judgment of those bad people out there?

- What do you make of Paul's assertion that all have sinned and fallen short of the glory of God? Is that an excessively pessimistic view of human nature? Do we in the church think too much about original sin and not enough about original blessing?

- How do you deal with difficult scriptural texts, perhaps passages that reflect different understandings on social issues, passages you don't like, passages that seem oppressive or unjust (e.g., clobber texts)?

- Where do you see the sin of idolatry at work in our world today? As part of your conversation with Scripture, read and reflect on a homily on modern day idolatry, offered by Pope Francis on October 15, 2013, which includes this insight:

> But since we all have need to worship—because we have the imprint of God within us—when we do not worship God, we worship creatures. And this is the passage from faith to idolatry. . . . We all have within ourselves some hidden idol. We can ask ourselves, in the sight of God: what is my hidden idol? What takes the place of God?"

Chapter Four

- As we come to the end of this section, we recognize that we each have to interpret the tradition in ways that make sense in our time. A billboard posted the statement: Jesus is the answer. Someone in graffiti wrote underneath: And what was the question? What do you think is the question that Jesus answers? After reading this section, who do you think Jesus is for Paul? How would you describe to someone your understanding of who Jesus is, and why he matters?

- Spend some time in consideration of these words that were so key to Paul's discussion:
  - Grace: What does grace mean? Where have you seen it at work? Have you experienced it in your own life? What does grace have to do with the story of Jesus?
  - Law: Is it a good thing or a bad thing? What would we do without it? What kinds of laws, rules, standards, expectations govern your life? Are you able to live up to them? What happens when you fall short of them? How did Jesus regard the laws of his own Jewish tradition?
  - Sacrifice: In what sense do you think that Jesus provides a sacrifice? Where and when have you experienced sacrificial giving? Is sacrifice a concept that belongs to a more primitive age?
  - Justification: What do you think it means to be justified? How much of that is God's work? How much of it is human work? In your mind, what does Jesus have to do with that work?
- Why do you think Paul spends time focusing on Abraham? What does Abraham have to teach us about faith? If you had to select a biblical character that helped you understand what faith is about, who would you describe? Are there people known to you outside of the biblical record who exhibit a faith you would wish to emulate?
- What are the pieces of tradition (like reference to Abraham) that help you to envision transformation?
- Reflect on the blessing that came to Abraham in Genesis 12:2–3:

  > I will make of you a great nation, and I will bless you, and make your name great, so that you will be a blessing. I will bless those who bless you, and the one who curses you I will curse, and in you all the families of the earth shall be blessed.

  - How do you understand this blessing in light of the passages we have been reading? Do you see it as a hopeful promise or not?

Chapter Five

- Reflect on the meaning of justification. Do you see it as God's work, or do you see it as something that you are responsible for? Is it something we need? If so, how do we access it?
- How does justification relate to reconciliation? Where have you seen the need for reconciliation in your relationship with God? In relationship with other people? Have you had the experience of reconciliation in your life? If so, how did it happen?
- What do you think Paul intends with the comparison of Adam and Christ? Talk about your impressions of the stories from the first chapters of Genesis, and why they may still be significant.
- Reflect on the power of law in your life. Paul's vision that human beings are captive to law may not seem relevant. But the idea that we are held captive by expectations of performance, by a sense of proving our own worth, by standards imposed by all kinds of societal institutions is timeless. The law may stand for any indicator of what we ought to be, demonstrating, perhaps illuminating, the ways we fall short. Reflect on Paul's experience described in chapter 7. Have you ever had a similar experience?
- Some might equate Paul's struggles (the end of chapter 7) with contemporary experience of addiction. What do you make of this quote from Nancy Van Dyke Platt and Chilton Knudsen in their short book *Depending on the Grace of God: A Spiritual Journey Through the Twelve Steps:*

> We must ask God for roadside assistance. Perhaps our understanding of God has gotten in the way of our efforts to free ourselves from addiction. Maybe we expected disappointment and judgment from God, or maybe we prayed for a miraculous rescue, in which God did all the work, and we were simply bystanders. The idea that God wants something better for us, created us for something good and free from addiction has not occurred to us before. We will work with God to become who we are created to be, free from dependency and addiction.[53]

117

- A great deal of Paul's letter has to do with the theme of hope. As Jim Wallis has said: "Hope is believing in spite of the evidence and watching the evidence change."[54] Or as Rob Bell says: "Love wins."[55] How would the church be different, how would our world be different, how would our individual lives and the interactions of the relationships of our lives be different if we really believed that there is nothing that can separate us from the love of God?

Chapter Six

- Paul has written about the importance of unity in the church. In the congregation where you worship, in your denomination, in ecumenical efforts, in discussions between conservative and progressive movements within the church, why is it important to focus on unity? What does it say about the church? What does it say about what the church believes? What are the catalysts that contribute to a sense of unity?
- It's been said that Sunday morning is the most segregated hour of the week in our culture. Racial divides are often most apparent when people gather to worship. What do you think Paul would have to say about that?
- How do you understand the mystery of faith? Why does faith seem to come to some people, and not to others? Where did your own faith come from?
- Chapters 9–11 have relevance for interfaith dialogue and especially for relationships between Christians and Jews. How does Paul's discussion inform that kind of dialogue? What problems does it address? What problems might it cause?
- Can we embrace the theocentric vision of this epistle with its claim of God's faithfulness, sovereignty, and mercy (even if we can't fully understand how those three things can be held at once)? For sure, we sense that those attributes are not yet fulfilled, not yet fully realized. We can cite all kinds of evidence that indicates that they have not yet been fulfilled. In light of that, where does faith enter into the discussion?
- When Paul says in 11:32 that God will show mercy to all, how broadly do you understand that word "all"?

▪ As Paul concludes these three chapters, he offers this hymn of praise:

> O the depth of the riches and wisdom and knowledge of God! How unsearchable are his judgments and how inscrutable his ways! "For who has known the mind of the Lord? Or who has been his counselor?" "Or who has given a gift to him, to receive a gift in return?' For from him and through him and to him are all things. To him be the glory for ever. Amen.

How do these verses inform our conversation with Scripture? What do they say about God? What do they say about us?

Chapter Seven

▪ Based on these last chapters of Paul's letter, how would you describe the new life that Paul believes has been brought about through the grace of God revealed in Jesus Christ? Reflect on the most important elements for you.

▪ Where do you see the church conformed to this world? Where do you see it transformed?

▪ How do you understand the phrase at the beginning of chapter 12 that speaks of the faithful way of life as spiritual worship? As a living sacrifice?

▪ Where do you see the spiritual gifts that Paul identifies in chapter 12 at work in your community? Do you see any of them in yourself?

▪ When Paul speaks of the place of Christians in the world in relationship to civic authorities, what part of his message translates into our own time as a guide? How does this passage (Romans 13:1–7) inform your own understanding of faithful citizenship? What is different between the context in which Paul wrote and our own?

▪ Reflect on the descriptions of those who are strong and those who are weak in the community. How would you describe what it means to be spiritually strong? How would you describe what it means to be weak? How does that square with Paul's words in 1 Corinthians: "My strength is made perfect in weakness" (KJV)? How does it square with Jesus's call to humility where he says that the first shall be last and the last shall be first?

■ In all of this discussion, how is it possible to build each other up in community? Where does that need to happen?

■ How do the personal references at the conclusion of this section in Romans, including those people receiving and sending greetings, deepen our understanding of the life of this congregation? Does it say anything to our communities of faith?

NOTES

Introduction to the Series

1. David F. Ford, "The Bible, the World and the Church I," in *The Official Report of the Lambeth Conference 1998,* ed. J. Mark Dyer et al. (Harrisburg, PA: Morehouse, 1999), 332.
2. For my broader understanding of authority, I am indebted to Eugene Kennedy and Sara C. Charles, *Authority: The Most Misunderstood Idea in America* (New York: Free Press, 1997).
3. William Sloane Coffin, *Credo* (Louisville, KY: Westminster John Knox Press, 2003), 156.

Autobiographical Note

4. William H. Willimon, *Shaped by the Bible* (Nashville: Abingdon Press, 1991), 10.

Chapter One

5. St. Augustine, *Confessions,* VIII, 12. (Oxford: Oxford Univ. Press).
6. Martin Luther, preface to *Latin Writings,* 1545. Translated by Bro. Andrew Thornton, OSB from the "Vorrede zu Band I der Opera Latina der Wittenberger Ausgabe. 1545" in vol. 4 of Luthers Werke in Auswahl, ed. Otto Clemen, 6th ed., (Berlin: de Gruyter, 1967), pp. 421–428.
7. John Webster, *Barth,* 2nd ed. (New York: Continuuum, 2004), 4.
8. Paul Tillich, *The Shaking of the Foundations* (New York: C. Scribner's Sons, 1948).
9. Ibid., pp. 161–162.
10. J. Christiaan Beker, *Paul the Apostle: The Triumph of God in Life and Thought* (Philadelphia: Fortress Press, 1984), 23ff.

11. James Carroll, *Constantine's Sword.* (London, New York: Houghton Mifflin, 2001).
12. From the Book of Common Prayer, Collect for the Sunday closest to November 16, Proper 28, p. 236.

Chapter Two

13. Karl Barth, *The Epistle to the Romans* (London, Oxford: Oxford University Press,1977), 42.
14. Karen Armstrong, interview with David Ian Miller, special to SFGate, www.sfgate.net, April 10, 2006.
15. Anders Nygren, *Commentary on Romans* (Philadelphia: Fortress Press, 1983), 67.
16. Tillich, from the sermon "You are accepted" in The *Shaking of the Foundations* (New York: C. Scribner's Sons. 1948), ch. 19.
17. C. K. Barrett, *The Epistle to the Romans* (New York: Harper and Row, 1957), 27.
18. Richard B. Hays, *Echoes of Scripture in the Letters of Paul* (New Haven, CT: Yale University Press, 1989), 37.
19. Ibid., 40.

Chapter Three

20. G. K. Chesterton, *Orthodoxy,* Chapter II, The Maniac. Project Gutenberg Ebook. Sept. 2005.
21. J. A. T. Robinson, *Wrestling with Romans* (Philadelphia: Westminster Press, 1979) 180.
22. Luke Timothy Johnson, *The Writings of the New Testament: An Interpretation* (Philadelphia: Fortress Press, 1986), 320.
23. Jim Hill and Rand Cheadle, *The Bible Tells Me So: The Uses and Abuses of Scripture* (New York: Anchor Books/Doubleday, 1996).

Chapter Four

24. *The Hymnal 1982* (New York: Church Publishing Inc.), hymn 686.
25. Ernst Käsemann, *Commentary on Romans* (Grand Rapids, MI: Wm. B. Eerdmans, 1980), 91–101.
26. Ibid., 93.
27. Johnson, *Writings of the New Testament,* 323.
28. Barrett, *Epistle to the Romans,* 81.
29. Nygren, *Commentary on the Romans,* 164.
30. Barrett, *Epistle to the Romans,* 86.

Chapter Five

31. C. S. Lewis, *Poems*. Walter Hooper, editor (New York: Mariner Books, 2002).
32. James Alison, *The Joy of Being Wrong: Original Sin Through Easter Eyes* (New York: Crossroads, 1998), 118–19.
33. Barrett, *Epistle to the Romans*, 111.
34. Bob Dylan, Gotta Serve Somebody, from Slow Train Coming, 1979 by Columbia Records.
35. Johnson, *Writings of the New Testament*, 327.
36. See endnote 34.

Chapter Six

37. Hymnal 1982, Hymn 469. (New York: Church Publishing Inc.)
38. Hays, *Echoes of Scriptures*, 64.
39. Ibid., 61.
40. Johnson, *Writings of the New Testament*, 333.
41. Hays, *Echoes of Scriptures*, 64.

Chapter Seven

42. Barrett, *Epistle to the Romans*, 230.
43. C. E. B. Cranfield, *Romans, A Shorter Commentary* (Grand Rapids, MI: Wm. B. Eerdman's Publ., 1985), 292.
44. Livy, *The History of Rome*, Books 1–5, translated with notes by Valerie M. Warrior (Indianapolis: Hackett Publishing, 2006), 122–123.
45. The Rule of St. Benedict, Chapter 53 (http://www.osb.org/rb/test/rbeaad1 .html#53).
46. Johnson, *Writings of the New Testament*, 334.
47. Barrett, *Epistle to the Romans*, 275.
48. From the Book of Common Prayer, p. 531, The Service for the Ordination of A Priest.
49. For other New Testament references to the role of deacon, see Acts 6:1–7, Phil.1:1, 1 Tim. 3:8–12).
50. For example, people like Timothy are mentioned (see Acts 16 and several other epistles for references to Timothy). Jason is mentioned in Acts 17:5–9. Sosipater, or Sopater, is mentioned in Acts 20:4 (again described as relative or compatriot). Tertius apparently serves as a scribe or secretary, a custom reflected in 1 Corinthians 16:21, Galatians 6:11, Colossians 4:18, and 2 Thessalonians 3:17. Gaius is noted as one who has shown hospitality (also mentioned in Acts 19:29, 20:4; 1 Cor. 1:14; 3 John 1:1). Erastus the city treasurer is mentioned in Acts 19:22 and 2 Timothy 4:20.

Chapter Eight

51. The General Thanksgiving from the Book of Common Prayer, p. 154.
52. Tillich, *The Shaking of the Foundations*, 162.

Study Questions

53. Nancy Van Dyke Platt and Chilton Knudsen, *Depending on the Grace of God* (Cincinnati, OH: Forward Movement, 2014), 6.
54. Jim Wallis, We all get healed, Program 4416, Air date: Nov. 21, 2000, or "The Power of Hope: A Sign of Transformation", *Sojourners Magazine*, Sept.–Oct. 1994.
55. Rob Bell, "Love Wins: A Book About Heaven, Hell and The Fate of Every Person Who Ever Lived" (New York: Harper One, 2011).

SUGGESTED READING

The Joy of Being Wrong, by James Alison. Crossroads. New York, 1998

A commentary on the *Epistle to the Romans*, C. K. Barrett. Harper and Row, Publishers, New York, c. 1957

The Epistle to the Romans, by Karl Barth. Translated from 6th edition by Edwyn C. Hoskyns. Oxford Univ. Press, London, Oxford, NY, 1977

Paul the Apostle: The Triumph of God in Life and Thought, by J. Christiaan Beker. Fortress Press, Philadelphia, PA, c. 1984

Paul's Apocalyptic Gospel: The Coming Triumph of God, by J. Christiaan Beker. Fortress Press, Philadelphia, PA, c. 1982

Constantine's Sword, by James Carroll. Houghton Mifflin, London and New York, 2001

Romans: A Shorter Commentary, C.E.B.Cranfield. Wm. B Eerdman's Publishing Company, Grand Rapids, MI, 1985

Spiritual Exercises Based on Paul's Epistle to the Romans, by Joseph A. Fitzmyer. S.J. Paulist Press, New York, 1995

Echoes of Scripture in the Letters of Paul, by Richard B. Hays. Yale Univ. Press, New Haven and London, c. 1989

The Bible Tells Me So: Uses and Abuses of Holy Scripture, by Jim Hill and Rand Cheadle. Anchor Books/Doubleday, New York, c. 1996

The Writings of the New Testament: An Interpretation, by Luke Timothy Johnson. Fortress Press, Philadelphia, PA, 1986

Commentary on Romans, by Ernst Kasemann. Wm. B Eerdmans Publishing Company, Grand Rapids, MI, c. 1980

The Shaking of the Foundations, by Paul Tillich. C. Scribner's Sons, New York, 1948

Commentary on Romans, by Anders Nygren. Fortress Press, Philadelphia, PA, 1983

Shaped by the Bible, by Will Willimon. Abingdon Press, Nashville, TN, 1990

BIOGRAPHY

The Rev. Jay Sidebotham is a graduate of Union Seminary in New York, and has served as a parish priest in the Episcopal Church since 1990. He presently directs a new ministry of Forward Movement called RenewalWorks. This work is committed to deeper spiritual growth in congregations. He also serves at a parish in Wilmington, NC, where he resides with his wife, Frances Murchison. He draws cartoons depicting church life and he finds no shortage of material.